SUMMARY AND D[...]

R.A. Banks, M.A., Ph.D.,
*Head of the Department of English and Drama, West London
Institute of Higher Education, Isleworth, Middlesex*

and

F.D.A. Burns, M.A., Ph.D.,
Head of the English Department, Newman College, Birmingham

HODDER AND STOUGHTON

LONDON SYDNEY AUCKLAND TORONTO

For:

Mary-Lou and Gwenfil Ann

Banks, Ronald Alfred
    Summary and directed writing.
    1. English language – Composition and exercises
    2. Abstracting – Problems, exercises, etc.
    I. Title   II. Burns, F D A
    428'2   PE1477
    ISBN 0 340 25608 7

First Published 1980. Fifth Impression 1982.

Printed and bound in Great Britain for
Hodder and Stoughton Educational,
a division of Hodder and Stoughton Ltd,
Mill Road, Dunton Green, Sevenoaks, Kent,
by Biddles Ltd, Guildford, Surrey

Introduction

This book explores some of the aspects of directed writing within the context of summarising skills. It sets out approaches to the selection of facts and details from passages and suggests some of the ways in which summarised material can be re-presented from one point of view rather than from another for a specific readership. It cannot provide a complete study of language 'registers', but it does provide opportunities to explore and use some of these registers.

All good writing (or speaking, for that matter) takes into account three essential things: (i) the viewpoint, attitude, or stance and purpose of the writer (or speaker); (ii) the nature of the body of ideas, facts, opinions, feelings, or arguments being presented; and (iii) the reader or the 'audience' at whom (or to whom) the writing or speaking is directed. The Assessment of Performance Unit's document, *Language Performance,* issued by the Department of Education and Science in May, 1978, set out this view of the nature of good writing as follows:

> Any use of language, whether spoken or written, implies that someone is seeking to convey meaning to someone else. In other words, there is always a context, about which we can ask, 'Who is saying (or writing) what, to whom, and why?'. The answers to these questions have important consequences for what can be said (or written) in a given context, and for how it can be said. Apart from the function that the language is intended to serve, the relationship between the speaker and the listener is especially significant. This is recognised in the concept of audience, i.e. the person (or persons) to whom an act of speech or writing is addressed.
>
> (*page* 5)

Much of the writing in schools or presented in examinations such as CSE or GCE has so far taken little account of this sense of 'audience'. It is often too readily assumed that the writing should be directed at the teacher or 'the examiner', whoever this strange disembodied creature may be. As a result the writing frequently lacks direction and fails to take account of contexts in which language is used. The same kind of 'neutral' writing has been expected of young writers whether they are expressing their own views about capital punishment or making a summary of the difficulties that someone else thinks a marine archaeologist meets as he works on sunken wrecks.

Personal responses to pictures and quotations, *or* narrative writing based on imagination or experience, *or* the presentation of a discussion of an important social issue, *or* a descriptive account of a process, a scene, or an event, *or* the development of a dramatic scene are important skills that need to be acquired and in all of them the three essential factors need to be borne in mind: the writer's viewpoint, the subject matter, and the audience or reader. It is, however, in the re-presentation of summarised material that these factors play a particularly important role.

To write effectively, then, it is important to be aware of the context in which language is being used and the more sensitive this awareness is, the more successful the writing is likely to be. There is no quick or easy way to acquire this sensitiveness; if it comes at all, it comes from extensive and close reading, the experience of using language in a variety of situations, response to different levels and varied kinds of writing, the critical examination of vocabulary, syntactical structures, and idiom in relation to meaning, and the discussion of implications and inferences to be drawn from the ordering and selection of ideas, figures of speech, and the choice of one word or expression rather than another. Such a sensitiveness will be developed by the critical study of, and response to, such things as, newspaper accounts of sporting activities, reports of political, military, or domestic events, editorials, and dramatic news items; magazine articles; the different language in text books on different subjects; lectures and debates; letters; passages from novels and critical writing; official reports and forms; dialogue; factual accounts; statistical data. It will come, above all, from using, reading, and listening to language within different contexts and on different levels and from noticing the differences that exist because of point of view, subject matter, and audience.

The first part of the book presents the basic skills needed for summary, together with some exercises drawn from recent GCE examinations; the second part provides a number of short exercises which are intended to encourage an awareness of language registers and usages; the third part consists of further exercises which combine summary and directed writing.

R.A.B.
F.D.A.B.

2

PART ONE

Summary

Section I

The skill to read a passage carefully, or to study an argument, or to examine a document closely, and then to extract from it details for a specific purpose is a useful one to acquire for our daily lives. This skill depends on the ability to read exactly what is on the page, to understand its meaning and significance within its own context, to recognize what is relevant and what is not, and to have some dexterity in arranging ideas coherently to produce a prescribed result.

The purpose of a summary may be to present ideas factually, to persuade others, to produce a balanced view of an argument, to amuse or interest, to explain, or to inform and instruct. The purpose needs to be clearly understood before the summary is attempted as it will determine the shape and form that the final draft will take.

The form of the summary may be that of a letter informally written to a relative or friend or one written formally to an employer, professional person, or an official. It is important that the appropriate and conventional forms of letter-writing are used, although the introductory headings and addresses ('the superscriptions', as they are sometimes called) and the concluding formulae ('the subscriptions') are not usually included in the total word-count maximum given in summary exercises.

The form may be that of a newspaper article and it will be readily obvious that the kind of writing used in one part of a newspaper (e.g. the editorial) may well differ substantially from that used in another (e.g. the sports pages). Candidates for public examinations in English Language which require a recognition of the different kind and levels of language appropriate for different contexts would be well advised to consider what some of the fundamental differences are between the language of one newspaper and that of another. A comparison between parts of a local paper and parts of a national 'quality' paper would be a valuable exercise.

Again, the form may be that of a 'report' and here some specific problems might be thought to arise. Some textbooks suggest specific lay-outs for reports, especially those to be written within the business world. There is always a formal quality about report-writing and ideally the form should be one normally found when a writer is presenting to a committee or an official or a colleague a statement which is essentially factual. However, provided the work is clearly and consistently arranged and the style is appropriate to a report the major attention of the report-writer should be to order his subject matter in as clear and as effective a manner as he can for a specific purpose.

Sometimes the form of the summary should be that of a speech or spoken discussion. Here it is important to recognize that spoken English differs in a number of important ways from that of written English. It would be helpful to study transcriptions of taped conversations and speeches to see the nature of some of these differences. Are there differences in sentence-construction, vocabulary, or idiom? How are ideas stressed? What use is made of rhetorical questions? How is the material arranged to produce the maximum impact on those listening? What effect does intonation have? (How does written English reflect intonation patterns?) What part does the audience have in determining the shape and the structure of the speech? These are a few of the questions to ask.

The form of the summary may be that of an article intended for a school or college magazine or a popular publication bought by young people. A careful investigation of some of the more noticeable features of the writing used would be helpful. How formal is the article? What use is made of 'I' and 'me', 'you', 'they' and 'them'? How technical can the vocabulary afford to be? What determines the order in which the material is presented? What assumptions, if any, can be specifically made about the intended reader? How would the style of the article have differed had it been prepared for another magazine?

A useful exercise, too, would be to examine your textbooks in the subjects you are studying. Does the language of the Geography book differ materially from that of the Physics book? How does an account of a battle in a History textbook differ from that of a battle in a novel? Most people would quickly recognize if the style of a book within a subject area was 'inappropriate', if the 'register' was wrong; it is not always as easy to describe the features of language which make it inappropriate. Nevertheless, it should be possible to experiment and to write the same material for a number of different contexts; this is a quick and enjoyable way to see whether you can recognize and use registers effectively.

The widely varied experience of close and alert reading and of using language on a number of different levels for specific contexts and audiences will be of immense value in writing summaries.

The basic skill, nevertheless, in producing a summary of a passage lies in the ability to select material accurately and relevantly. This selection is best approached systematically:

1   It is important that the sense of the text and the viewpoint of the writer are established by a *first* careful reading. Conclusions about these matters should be tested by a *second* detailed reading to confirm or to modify them.

2   Summary exercises normally prescribe exactly what material should be selected. The passage should be read a *third* time and detailed notes made on the areas prescribed. These notes are most useful if they are scrupulously accurate and **not** in the words of the original passage. Some words or expressions cannot be economically replaced and it is acceptable to retain them.

3   Once the material has been selected it should be arranged and grouped in the most effective way to allow for the 'slanting' of it towards a particular 'audience' or group of readers.

4   These notes should then be checked against the original text in order to make sure that they accurately reflect its meaning. This *fourth* reading should ensure that no relevant information has been omitted.

5   Any notes which retain the wording of the original should be checked against the text in order to see if they might not be paraphrased accurately and economically. At this stage a count of the number of words in the notes should be made to ensure that any maximum word-limit can be observed as the final work is drafted.

6   Now it is essential to refer once more to the rubric which states how and where the material should be directed, in order to adopt the right form and the appropriate 'register'.

The writing-up of the selected material is of the utmost importance in an exercise which combines summary with directed writing.

7   The form (e.g. letter, dialogue, report, article, etc.) should be meticulously and consistently observed. The appropriate 'register' (i.e. the appropriate form of language for the context) must be maintained; this will require a judicious use of vocabulary, attention to sentence-construction, and an ability to distinguish the appropriate from the inappropriate. The rubric normally asks candidates to write accurately and special care should be taken with grammar, syntax, and punctuation.
A draft should be made from the notes without any reference

back to the original which might lead to the introduction of words and expressions from the original text. The word-length of the draft should be checked and adjusted, if necessary. The prescribed length should never be exceeded and any shortfall merely makes it difficult to include all the necessary material.

8   The final version can now be written up and then checked to see that the writing is clear, accurate, and appropriate. At this stage it is still permissible to make amendments and alterations provided that they are clear and leave the writing legible. There is no need to write a 'fair copy'.

9   The exact number of words used should now be placed at the end of the draft to be assessed.

The major fault in the summary exercise all too frequently is the failure by candidates to select *enough relevant* material. Inadequate details and the inclusion of garbled or irrelevant ideas or information waste words and mar the final draft. It is usually helpful in the preparation of notes to check every sentence of the original text during the fourth reading to see if it contributes in any way to the argument of the summary; sentences should be rejected only if they can be clearly shown to have no bearing whatsoever on this argument.

Exercises in the selection of material for summaries

EXERCISE ONE

Do not write out the final summary. This exercise is concerned with the selection of material and the preparation of notes only.

The following passage is taken from an article dealing with changes in village life. *Using only the information given in the passage,* **make notes** for a summary to be written in two paragraphs as follows:

a the social structure of village life in the past; *and*

b the pattern of village life today.

Select the material you need and arrange it in a sensible order within the notes for the appropriate paragraph. *Write in clear and correct English. Use your own words as far as possible,* but some words and expressions cannot be accurately or economically replaced.

The notes for your summary should not exceed 150 words altogether; *at the end of your notes state the exact number of words you have used.*

Perhaps one of the reasons underlying the success of 'The Archers' as a popular radio serial is that the everyday picture of country life which it presents takes some account of the fact that the world of the village evolves gradually; its changes are rarely sudden or dramatic
5 but they are relentless and irresistible.
    The social structure of the English village, even half a century or so ago, was clearly defined and established according to an easily understood hierarchy based on position or occupation. At the head was the squire or the aristocratic inhabitant of the 'great house'. Then
10 there came a miscellaneous group of gentry, often retired and sometimes relatives of landed families in the county; in this group the village parson must be included. There followed in the scheme of things the large farmers and below them the school teacher, the farm bailiff, the shop-keepers, and certain skilled craftsmen. Finally there
15 were the smallholders and then the workers who had their own occupational prestige scale according to their jobs: shepherd, ploughman, cowman, pig-keeper, and farm-hand.
    The 'great house' and its family was no doubt an object of respect and a source of bounty. Deference was demanded – and received –

20 from tenants and cottagers whose livelihood was partly dependent on the goodwill of the owner. Many of the working-class laboured on the estate or in the house itself and this dependence inculcated attitudes of respect. The aristocrat and his family were often completely ignorant of local affairs and surrounded by hangers-on.

25 Today, however, the squire is more likely to be sitting on the magistrates' bench and aware of the social problems that help to cause delinquency or, as a member of the local council, taking an active interest in housing the poor, providing better social amenities, or offering services to the aged. His own social position, nevertheless,

30 is being challenged in today's changing world.

The parson is still there but his position, too, has altered. He has to look after many parishes and his former lucrative living is no longer comfortable as inflation grows and his benefice remains constant. He cannot rely on his former status or income as rector or vicar and finds

35 it impossible to maintain much of an appearance in the community, as he crouches in an enormous rectory, helps his wife with the washing-up, and worries about the cost of heating and cleaning such a vast mansion.

The changing life of the village is perhaps best reflected in the life

40 of the farm-worker. His improved general education, his higher wages negotiated by a powerful trade union, his working hours that are permanently fixed, and his more humane conditions of service reveal a different attitude towards the lot of the labourer. Not so long ago he was expected to live in sub-standard housing, accept

45 depressed wages as his lot, and, without thought of changing employment, devote the whole of his life and energies to the needs of one farm, where he counted himself fortunate to be employed. Hours of work were not reckoned, holidays were neither offered nor expected, and machines were not available to relieve him of

50 drudgery. Cows had to be milked; sheep were not clock-watchers in the lambing season; and a fine light evening could not be idly spent when there was a harvest to be brought in. Today the farm-worker has a standard working-week beyond which he calculates his overtime as readily and easily as the factory-worker on a car-

55 production line.

EXERCISE TWO

Do not write out the final summary. This exercise is concerned with the selection of material and the preparation of notes only.

The following passage is taken from an article dealing with the life of children and attitudes to them in the seventeenth and eighteenth centuries. *Using only the information given in the passage,* **make notes** for a summary to be written in two paragraphs as follows:

a the life of children and the attitude of adults towards them in the seventeenth century; *and*

b the life of children and the attitude of adults towards them in the eighteenth century.

Select the material you need and arrange it in a sensible order within the notes for the appropriate paragraph. *Write in clear and correct English. Use your own words as far as possible,* but some words and expressions cannot be accurately or economically replaced.

The notes for your summary should not exceed 150 words altogether; *at the end of your notes state the exact number of words you have used.*

There were some parents in the seventeenth century who were so ignorant about their children that they did not even know how many children they had; it surprises us to learn that many could bury their children without feeling very much emotion at all. For the majority of
5 families there was a coldness, almost a callousness, in the relationship between parents and children. Almost as soon as they were born, babies were stretched out on a board and bound tightly in swaddling clothes so that they could not move and become a nuisance to those around them. They were changed very infrequently and often they
10 were sent out to a wet-nurse, who might have as many as five or six babies to look after. She was likely to live in a home alive with dirt and disease. It is not surprising, therefore, that one in four children died before the age of one and at least fifty per cent of children died before they reached their teens.
15 With the turn of the century child mortality, though still high, began to decrease, partly because of a steadily increasing food supply and partly because the scourge of smallpox was gradually being eliminated. Parents began to devote more of their time to their children and they had more money to spend on them. Public opinion

20 about the upbringing and punishment of children also began to
change. For instance, following Locke's work on education, by 1700
opinion began to move gradually against the merciless flogging and
beating of children. Everybody had believed that human nature was
basically wicked and sinful and that the best way to keep evil down
25 was to whip the child regularly to instil in him subservience and the
willingness to obey; very few escaped the rod for long.

All these developments helped to create a new world for children.
In the seventeenth century you expected your children to follow the
trade you had grown up in. In the eighteenth century there were all
30 sorts of new and exciting economic opportunities for the child of
skilled workers who managed to get just a little education.

Naturally when such parents began to spend their money on their
offspring they spent it first of all to give them a better start in life.
They tended to use an increasing part of their resources on books, on
35 schools, and on things which would improve their child's chance of
getting on in life; so we see the change first taking effect in the
contents of what a child read in school. In the seventeenth century
there had been very few books designed especially for children; there
were school books, but they were very difficult to comprehend
40 without learning by rote. They were not made to attract the eye of a
child. This began to change about 1740 when a publisher called
Newbury began to produce books with attractive drawings especially
for small children. Books of this kind rapidly proliferated and by the
end of the eighteenth century there were hundreds of titles every year
45 of new children's books, often beautifully illustrated and teaching
almost everything that there was to be taught. It was not only the
children of the middle classes who could enjoy this literature, because
publishers realized that those of less affluent parents formed just as
promising a market. So they began to issue books in parts, children's
50 encyclopaedias published part by part at a penny a week – a practice
which has its modern counterparts and imitators.

There was also a development in toys. In the seventeenth century
the children had very few toys indeed and these were made without
any sophistication. But from 1730 onwards the shrewd shopkeepers
55 began to realize that parents were willing to spend money on well-
made toys, particularly those which would help educate a child, such as
toy looms which could be dismantled and reconstructed, model
farmyards, playing cards designed to teach the alphabet, and the
jigsaw puzzle, a British invention, which was devised to teach
60 children geography.

EXERCISE THREE

Do not write out the final summary. This exercise is concerned with the selection of material and the preparation of notes only.

The following passage is taken from an article on the packaging of goods. *Using only the information given in the passage,* **make notes** for a summary to be written in two paragraphs as follows:

a the advantages of modern packaging; *and*

b the problems caused by modern packaging.

You should not attempt to summarise everything there is in the passage, but should select from it only the material you need for your notes.

Write in clear and correct English and *use your own words as far as possible,* although you may retain words and expressions which cannot be accurately or economically replaced.

The notes for your summary should not exceed 140 words altogether; *at the end you must state accurately the number of words you have used.*

Almost everything bought nowadays has to be broken out of its box, packet, tube, carton or tin before it can be used. Non-returnable wrappings impose serious strains on local authorities, whose responsibility it is to collect and dispose of our rubbish. Ratepayers
5 have to find the 50 million pounds annually required to deal with the processing of 14 million tons of refuse. The destruction of waste is also difficult, as much of the packaging we use consists of materials which stubbornly refuse to be broken down naturally by decomposition. Expensive incinerators have to be installed and the
10 smoke they produce causes some pollution of the atmosphere. Packaging, too, in the form of litter spoils the environment we all share, whether it is in the town, in the countryside, or on the beach.
Industry and selling agencies, however, continue to introduce more and more packaging every week. One large agency argues its
15 views without the trace of an apology: cigarettes, wrapped in tinfoil and placed in a box, which is then wrapped in cellophane, retain their flavour better and have a longer shelf-life than products less carefully packaged; products sold in jars are protected from the contamination which would be bound to occur if they were handled continually by
20 shop assistants or, in self-service stores, by intending purchasers. The

higher cost of wrapping goods carefully is reflected in their higher prices, but money spent on ensuring greater freshness and the higher standard of hygiene achieved by good wrapping is money well spent.

25 The housewife, surrounded by clamouring young children, needs to be able to make her purchases both quickly and economically. Packing goods in such a way that their price and weight are seen at a glance will help her to make her choice. Some unscrupulous manufacturers may try to deceive her by increasing the size of a carton whilst reducing the quantity of its contents, or by changing the

30 shape of a bottle in order to conceal the fact that it contains fewer fluid ounces or cubic centimetres; but recent attempts to standardize packet sizes by introducing 'Eurosizes' help to make the housewife's task easier. Uniformity in the size of packets also leads to quicker transporation and more efficient display and storage of goods. If

35 marketing costs are held down, some of the savings can be passed on to the consumer in the form of stabilized prices. Not everyone approves of standardization, however. Colourful wrappings do make goods look attractive and provide variety; they can stimulate a healthy demand, which leads to increased competition between

40 manufacturers and the maintenance of employment for the workers in the companies.

Those who watch over the interests of the consumer sometimes argue that wrappings are unnecessarily complicated and merely serve to confuse the shopper; it is difficult to compare accurately in the

45 bustle of a supermarket the value of a pear-shaped bottle of shampoo containing 1300 ccs and sold for 35p with that of a round-shaped bottle containing 1650 ccs and sold for 42p. To make the necessary comparisons a housewife needs a pocket calculator and an escape from her clamouring children. In the end the article will sell on the

50 strength of its attractive packaging. Only when she reaches the check-out will she realize just how bulky the cartons, bottles, and tins have made her shopping; two journeys to the shops will be necessary instead of the one she made in the days when packaging was less elaborate.

55 Nevertheless, anything which helps to brighten our lives is worthwhile. The merest suggestion on a packet that we shall be fitter, more loved, richer, or happier if we buy the product will lure us to spend more than we can afford and ignore the blatant waste of the earth's resources in the making of unnecessary boxes, packets, tubes,

60 cartons and tins.

EXERCISE FOUR

Do not write out the final summary. This exercise is concerned with the selection of material and the preparation of notes only.

The following extract is taken from a discussion at a school council meeting on discipline. Mrs Anstey and Mr Jackson are teachers and Anne and John are in their last year at school. *Using only the information given in the passage,* **make notes** for a summary to be written in two paragraphs as follows:

a ways of producing good behaviour in schools, *and*

b the consequences for pupils of their bad behaviour.

You should not try to summarise everything there is in the passage, but should select from it only the material you need for your notes.

Write in clear and correct English and *use your own words as far as possible,* although you may retain words and brief expressions which cannot be accurately or economically replaced.

The notes for your summary should not exceed 150 words altogether; *at the end of it you must state accurately the number of words you have used.*

Mrs Anstey:	Discipline in schools is generally good. In many the children are working well and happily. Shall we turn to some of the things which help boys and girls to behave well in school?
5 *Anne:*	Everything depends on what the school expects of the pupils. If it expects us to behave responsibly, then we will; if it expects us to behave badly we'll react that way.
John: 10	There's more to it than that! When I was younger I knew that I should be put into detention or be sent to the headmaster if I broke the rules. Some were even caned or suspended for bad behaviour.
Mrs Anstey: 15	I'm sure it makes for good behaviour if there is a feeling of pride in belonging to a particular form or in being a member of a certain school. I know that in my own form there is a very strong spirit; no-one wants

to misbehave, because it lets everyone else down
and takes away the class's good name.

John: They don't misbehave, because they know that Mrs
Anstey will see their parents if they do – and they
don't want to get into trouble with their mothers
and fathers!

Anne: Parents have enough worries of their own. They like
to see their sons and daughters winning prizes or
getting good marks for homework. Rewards like
these encourage pupils to work and behave
properly.

Mrs Anstey: They also need something to aim at – passing an
examination or getting into a university or finding a
good job. These are the incentives which make boys
and girls study hard and behave well.

John: It's all very well for you, Mrs Anstey, to say that,
but when you're young you don't understand. Some
teachers shout at the class when we misbehave and
this spoils the lesson for us. Yet I remember one of
my primary school teachers who made us behave
properly because we would have done anything to
avoid being shouted at by her. She never used the
cane or kept us in; she didn't need to.

Mr Jackson: Teachers don't like shouting either; it gives them
headaches. The real secret, I think, lies in children
being interested in what they are doing. Bored
children are the ones who get into trouble; if they
are busy they have no desire to get up to mischief.

Anne: The thing I hated most was being sent out of the
room if I misbehaved. It meant that I was losing
valuable lesson time and falling behind the others.

Mrs Anstey: No other reason?

Anne: I suppose that I was afraid that Mr Cairns, the
headmaster, would come along and catch me
outside. He might then have regarded me as a
troublemaker and written bad testimonials to stop
me from getting a good job when I left school.

John: When we misbehaved he used to cancel our games
days. Do you remember that he banned the sixth-

14

	form discos for a whole term when someone broke a projector and wouldn't own up?
Mr Jackson:	You must expect to lose your pleasures and privileges if you misbehave; that's what happens in the adult world, after all, where fines and imprisonment are used.
Mrs Anstey:	That's a negative way of looking at things. We all know when we work well and behave with consideration for others; this knowledge, in itself, is its own reward; it brings with it its own feeling of contentment and satisfaction. This, in turn, helps us to behave well.
Mr Jackson:	Be that as it may, is there anything we can do as a school council?
Anne:	We can make pupils behave properly by using our own authority. Last year we made the third form – I think it was your class, Mrs Anstey – repair the damage and clean up the mess they had caused one wet lunch hour. The sight of that room would have made the cleaners come out on strike!
Mrs Anstey:	It most certainly was not my form! It was Mr Jackson's!

EXERCISE FIVE

Do not write out the final summary. This exercise is concerned with the selection of material and the preparation of notes only.

The following extract is taken from a study of gangs. *Using only the information given in the passage,* **make notes** for a summary to be written in one paragraph on:

> the main characteristics of gangs.

You should not try to summarise everything there is in the passage, but should select from it only the material you need for your notes.

Write in clear and correct English and *use your own words as far as possible,* although you may retain words and brief expressions which cannot be accurately or economically replaced.

The notes for your summary should not exceed 130 words altogether; *at the end you must state accurately the number of words you have used.*

Between the ages of twelve and fourteen young people enter what the psychologists and sociologists like to call 'the gang phase', when many of them form into gangs. Earlier in their lives, children form groups which consist of both boys and girls but gangs are never mixed. They
5 consist exclusively either of boys or of girls.
The strongest feature of a gang is, perhaps, its bond of unswerving allegiance to the group; to become a member is to accept this unspoken bond without question. Newcomers are allowed to join only if they are prepared to agree to this and frequently only after
10 having passed some kind of admission test to prove their loyalty, courage, sincerity, toughness, or whatever qualities are thought important for the well-being and survival of the gang.
One gang may be held together by an interest or pastime that all its members share, such as football, going to dances, robbing orchards,
15 or beating up rival gangs. Another may be held together by nothing more than a simple impulse to come together. You can see this instinct at work on a Saturday or Sunday afternoon in those gang-members who wander about with no common interest other than a certain satisfaction in being with others. It has been known for a gang
20 to remain together because of a common grudge from which they imagine they all suffer: the rejection of them by their parents or teachers; their unjustified persecution by those in authority,

especially the police; or their being attacked by other racial or
political groups.

25   It is sometimes argued that adolescents are naturally rebellious and
unwilling to carry out instructions and this may well be true of their
attitude towards those whose authority they fail to recognize. Yet,
strangely, obedience and not rebelliousness is the law of the gang. In
point of fact, adolescents are extremely obedient and submissive –
30 but only to their accepted leader, whether this be someone their own
age or an adult. It is essential that the leader should be one of
themselves and should understand and struggle to meet the needs of
the group as a whole. It is these things which distinguish a leader from
a dictator: a dictator governs from the outside, he orders, and he
35 commands. Significantly some teachers are regarded as dictators and
others as leaders!

    Although loyalty to the leader must be accepted, in belonging to a
gang members need not lose their own individualities. Indeed, their
value to the gang itself may well rest in their ability to contribute
40 something to it which no one else can: they may be especially gifted at
dancing, singing, climbing trees, throwing tin cans accurately, or
hurling abuse. Provided they do not commit the sin of showing-off
or challenging the authority of the leader, the gang will give its
approval to their individual contributions. It may be argued that in
45 offering their talents to the community which they have freely joined
they have kept their individuality.

    For parents to insist that their child should dress differently or be
treated differently from others in the gang may bring humiliation and
unpopularity upon him, as he must, if he is to remain a member, keep
50 to the unwritten law of the gang which demands a uniform of some
kind. The dress of the 'Teddy Boys', 'Rockers', 'Greasers', or 'Hell's
Angels' is slavishly adopted by members of these groups because
acceptance of it denotes their acceptance of the gang itself and the
gang's acceptance of them; in a way it is a sign of membership
55 recognized by everyone.

    As boys and girls are loyal to their own gangs, so they are hostile to
all other gangs, whom they regard as their natural enemies. They can
be very cruel, too, not only to rival groups, but to individuals outside
their gang as well – to the boy who is too tall or useless at sport, or to the
60 girl who stammers or suffers from acne. It is unjust and it is cruel, but
this behaviour is a common feature of gangs.

    Eventually the gang spirit, rightly exercised, passes into adult social
and communal life. Our clubs, our churches, and our political parties
are developments of the social impulse and show many of the
65 characteristics of the 'gangs' of our youth.

Summary

Section II

In another type of summary set in public examinations, candidates are sometimes required to grasp the sense of a whole passage and to express it in accurate, continuous prose in normally about a third of its original length. For this exercise, a number of approaches can usefully be borne in mind.

1 The passage will usually present a logical argument set out in a number of stages. It is important to identify and include each stage.

2 Each stage or point of the argument is likely to be supported by examples and illustrations. The general idea needs to be separated from the specific example, for there is no room in such a summary for a minor detail. Where there are several examples given together, it is often possible to generalize the main point they illustrate from them.

3 Students are expected to use their own words as far as possible in order to show an understanding of the original passage which would not be apparent from copying. This does not mean, however, that all the words have to be replaced. The skill lies in identifying key words central to the argument which could not be more briefly expressed without a loss in accuracy.

4 An important part of the preparation of such a summary is the making (and numbering) of clear notes. These should be direct and yet full enough to support a final draft.

5 Continuity and fluency are important to the final summary and can frequently be achieved through the use of brief linking words. Where possible, use the tense of the original passage; it is not always desirable to write in the past tense.

6 It is always assumed in such a summary that the student is writing for a teacher or examiner. It is therefore best to retain the tone of the original writing as far as possible.

7 Always state at the end of the summary the number of words used. It can be assumed that whoever set the task has been able to write a full summary using somewhat fewer words than the maximum allowed in an examination.

EXERCISE SIX

For practice, *prepare a list of notes* which could form the basis for a summary of the whole of the following passage on the Namib Desert. Number each note. The passage contains 344 words and *your notes should not be more than 100 words.* (A continuous summary from these notes would need to use not more than 120 words.)

At the end of this book you will find a list of notes on this passage (page 125) from which a summary might be written. Notes will vary from person to person and there is no such thing as a 'model answer'. You would find it useful to check your notes *once you have made them* against those given on page 125.

Picture a sea of red sand 500 miles wide, running alongside one of the wildest oceans in the world. The 'waves' in that sand sea are mostly 1,000 feet high, with some topping the 1,200 foot mark, the highest in the world. They are in the Namib Desert in south-west Africa, a most
5 beautiful place with its shapes and colour and spectacular changes of light. By mid-morning the sun beats down raising the surface temperature of those dunes to over 62 degrees Centigrade, far too hot for the naked foot to touch. It never rains in the Namib. The combination of heat and perpetual drought makes it impossible to
10 imagine that anything can live there. Yet climb one of those dunes – in the cool of the evening – and you discover that the Namib is far from empty of life. The red sand is marked by thousands of strange tracks: small circles of footprints made by beetles; long squiggly signatures of a lizard's tail; a series of loops made by a side-winder viper; and,
15 at the foot of the dunes, the immense marks of a fast-moving animal, the oryx. Though you may have seen no living creature, it is obvious that the Namib is teeming with life.

How can these many species exist in such a hostile environment? No matter how adapted to desert living, almost every creature needs
20 moisture. The Namib Desert starts its day, quite unbelievably, wrapped in dense grey fog that often extends fifty miles back into the dunes from a shoreline dreaded by sailors as the 'Skeleton Coast'. Towering surf crashes on to its sands, while a few hundred yards offshore runs a cold Antarctic current called the Benguella. The
25 meeting of superheated air from the desert with the chilly atmosphere above the Benguella each morning produces this pall of fog which leaves heavy droplets of water on sand, rocks, and the sparse vegetation. Almost every creature that has learned to live in the Namib does so because it has discovered how to make use of this daily delivery
30 of water.

EXERCISE SEVEN

Make notes which could form the basis for a summary of the whole of the following passage on children's street games. Number each note. The passage contains 349 words and *your notes should not be more than 110 words in length.*

When children play in the street they not only avail themselves of one of the oldest play-places in the world; they engage in some of the oldest and most interesting of games, for they are games tested and confirmed by centuries of children, who have played them and passed
5 them on, as children continue to do, without reference to print, parliament, or adult propriety. Indeed these street games are probably the most played, least recorded, most natural games that there are. Certainly they are the most spontaneous, for the little group of boys under the lamp-post may not know, until a minute
10 before, whether they are to play 'Bish Bash' or 'Cockarusha', or even know that they are going to play.
   A true game is one that frees the spirit. It allows of no cares but those fictitious ones engendered by the game itself. When the players commit themselves to the rhythm and incident of 'Underground Tig'
15 or 'Witches in the Gluepots', they opt out of the ordinary world; the boundary of their existence becomes the two pavements this side of a pillar-box, their only reality the excitement of avoiding the chaser's touch. Yet it is not only the nature of the game that frees the spirit; it is the circumstances in which it is played. The true game is one that
20 arises from the players themselves.
   It may even be argued that the value of a game as recreation depends on its inconsequence to daily life. In the games which adults organise for children, the outside world is ever present. Individual performances tend to become a matter for congratulation or shame;
25 and in a team game, paradoxically, individual responsibility presses hardest. The player who 'lets down his side' can cheer himself only with the sad reflection that those who speak loudest about the virtues of organised sport are the people who excel in it, never the duffers. He is not likely to have been told that such a man as Robert Louis
30 Stevenson felt that cricket and football were colourless pastimes, compared with the romance of Hide and Seek.

EXERCISE EIGHT

Compose notes which could be used to write a summary of the following passage on sunken ships. Number each note. The passage contains 349 words, and *your notes should not be more than 110 words in length.*

More ships have sunk around the coasts of Britain than around those of any other country in the world. Although this is hardly a record to be proud of, it is historical fact. So much so that it is almost impossible to stand on a stretch of our coastline and look out over the
5 sea without viewing, unknowingly, the graveyard of at least a dozen ships. A map of school-atlas size, for example, when used to plot all the wrecks from Cornwall to the Thames Estuary, ends up with just a mass of shading along the coast – even when each wreck is marked with the tiniest cross. Along other coasts, though the picture is
10 often not so dark, it is difficult to find any area where a sinking has not taken place. Remember, too, that these are only the recorded wrecks. What casualties were suffered in the earliest days of our maritime history can be estimated only from fragments of the earliest writings. The more ancient, less seaworthy vessels must have suffered
15 even more.

    The British Isles have been a centre for trade from earliest times. We have sent out ships and ships have come to us. Whether for trade, exploration, or war, ships have sailed to and from these islands for thousands of years. During that time the weather and other natural
20 hazards have taken a steady toll. Many of these lost ships went down laden with exotic cargo – with ivory, diamonds, gold, silver, pearls, silk, and all manner of costly things. Just as many sank full of coal, vegetables, corn, iron ore, rubber, petrol, hides, and ammunition, or less deadly general goods, from pianos to cement. Once sunk their
25 story might have ended, unless, of course, the professional divers with their leaden boots and globe helmets were called in for some prize of exceptional value. But even these tough, experienced men were used only if the exact location of the wreck were known or could be found with ease. It took the invention of the Aqualung in 1944 to make free-
30 ranging over the seabed in search of wrecks a possibility.

mundane cargoes too

EXERCISE NINE

Write notes from which a summary of the following passage on zoos could be written. Number your notes. The passage contains 348 words; *do not use more than 110 words in your notes.*

120

There are now almost five hundred zoos and aquaria scattered throughout the world. In an average year their turnstiles click some 333 million times. A great many clicks represent repeated visits by keen zoo-goers and members of zoo societies, but these figures
5 indicate that at least a twentieth of the world's entire population goes to a zoo once or more every year.

There cannot be many other institutions whose appeal is as universal, for, if we look at the figures for world zoo attendances, we find that the eight highest are in seven different countries. Why do so
10 many people visit zoos? In some parts of Asia and Latin America, it may be partly because there are not many rival attractions such as museums, art galleries, and theatres. In many places it may be partly because it costs so little. Nobody pays to visit the Mexico City zoo, while the San Diego zoo is free to all under seventeen, and the Peking
15 zoo to everyone under a metre tall. But cheapness and lack of rival attractions go only a little way towards explaining the immense popularity of zoos.

The simple fact is that people all over the world love animals and have an immense curiosity about them. The ordinary citizen, with no
20 specialized knowledge of animals, may see more different species in a single day at the zoo than he could find by searching the globe for several years. What is more, he can usually see them in the delightful surroundings of well-laid-out gardens. More often than not there are guide-books or notices to tell him something about the habits of each
25 species and what part of the world it comes from, so that he can furnish his mind as he feasts his eyes. However, to give pleasure and entertainment to the public is an important but secondary aim of zoos. Man began to study animals while he was still living in caves, and he is likely always to go on doing so. The essential purpose of a
30 zoo is thus to provide special opportunities for this study.

EXERCISE TEN

Write notes which could form the basis of a summary of the following passage on journalism. The passage contains 346 words. Number your notes and *do not use more than 110 words.*

Journalism is a popular choice with young people seeking an interesting career. Each year several thousands apply to editors for a job; about six hundred are successful. So competition for the available openings is keen. What will an editor be looking for in his
5 new recruits? First, he will want young people with a sound education. If you can also write shorthand – or are learning to do so – an editor will almost certainly grant you an interview. Examination successes alone are never a reliable guide to suitability for journalism. An editor will want to make sure you have the right personality too.
10 A journalist has to meet, talk with and gain the confidence of all sorts and conditions of men. He must be able to deal with the humble and meek without being patronising and the mighty without an inhibiting deference. He must be persistent without blustering or bullying; he must neither intimidate nor be intimidated; he must be sympathetic
15 without being gullible, sceptical without becoming a cynic.
    He must also have an inquiring mind. All through his life, the journalist is asking: 'Why?' Why did this happen? Why did this man do that? He must have news-sense. This is unlikely to be highly developed in beginners, but anyone who wants a career in journalism
20 should be sufficiently interested to discover for himself what makes news and how it is expressed. It it important too that he should have opinions of his own, although the first lesson he must learn is to subjugate his own views and to conduct an interview or record a speech without revealing his agreement or disagreement with the
25 subject matter. But he will make a poor job of it if he has no personal convictions.
    What about writing ability? It is, of course, essential but, without the other qualities mentioned, it is of little use to a newspaper reporter. Finally, the would-be journalist must be prepared to work
30 erratic hours, sometimes under intense pressure. If he is really 'born to it', he will endure this and even enjoy it.

PART TWO

Directed Writing

The purpose of the exercises in this part of the book is to provide experience in 'directing' or 'slanting' writing for a particular 'audience' or reader. The use of the correct 'registers' (the appropriate language for the context) and the use of a correct form are essential.

The exercises are based on various kinds of writing. You are not expected to use all the facts or information they contain or to imitate the angle from which the passage was originally written. Select only those details you need for your purpose, elaborating on them or responding to them as you judge necessary; arrange them as effectively as you can and re-present them in an appropriate form and in appropriate language.

EXERCISE ELEVEN

Imagine that friends of yours are trying to set up their own pop group, and they need bookings and engagements. You have agreed to write a hand-out which can bring them publicity and be sent to organisers of dances and pop concerts as well as local newspapers.

You have the following details to work on:

Name of Group: Sounds Right

Members:
1   Mike Daley   Lead guitarist
    (Studying classical music at college.)

2   Dave Satch   Rhythm guitarist
    (Has provided background support for other groups during recording sessions at a local recording studio.)

3   Frank Singleton   Synthesiser and also Electric Organ
    (Trained in playing the piano from the age of eight. Interested in electronics.)

4   George Bright   Drums
    (His father was a professional drummer with a large band in the 1950s.)

5   Mary Mackie   Lead vocal
    (Solo soprano singer at school concerts.)

Type of Music: Mod to Soul music.

Repertoire: Music for listening to or dancing to. Able to imitate and adapt 'top of the pops' tunes.

Previous Appearances: Regular Friday evening performances at a local youth club. One appearance on local television.

Equipment: Fully equipped with amplifiers and speaker cabinets for a large hall. Able to set up a sound to light system.

Transport: Bedford van, driver Mike Daley.

Fee:	Variable. Negotiated according to type of performance required.
Bookings:	Contact Frank Singleton (Phone 1234)

Making use of the details given, adding to them where necessary, and relating them to your locality, *write a publicity leaflet for the group.*

EXERCISE TWELVE

The following notes provide information about the life and works of Mother Teresa. Using some or all of the information, write an informative article about Mother Teresa (for publication in your school or college magazine) in which you convey your admiration for what she has done.

A Roman Catholic Missionary working in India.

A small slight woman, remarkable for her energy, her humour and her humility.

Born 17 August, 1910, in Skopje, Yugoslavia.

5 At the age of eighteen joined the Sisters of Loretto in Dublin where she studied English. Sent to an Indian hill station at Darjeeling.

Taught geography at St Mary's High School, Calcutta. Became Principal of the School.

On 10 September, 1946, received 'a call within a call'.

10 'The message was quite clear. I was to leave the convent and help the poor whilst living among them. It was an order. I knew where I belonged, but I did not know how to get there.'

On 16 August, 1948, left the convent for the streets and slums of Calcutta. In 1950 founded the Missionaries of Charity.

15 Since then she has been responsible for setting up many schools, orphanages and houses for the poor in India and other countries. In 1952 she set up the Nirmal Hriday Home for Dying Destitutes in Calcutta. Other centres include an orphanage for abandoned children, a colony for lepers, a home for the elderly and bewildered, a
20 workshop for the unemployed. At least eighty-five centres established in India. Sixty-five branches of the mission now operate more than a hundred children's homes.

Projects range from more houses for the destitute and dying to work with drug addicts and alcoholics.

25 Awarded the Pope John XXIII Peace Prize 1971.

Awarded the Nobel Peace Prize 1979.

EXERCISE THIRTEEN

The following letters are taken from magazines for young people, and each expresses worry and concern about a particular problem. Imagine that you are the adult to whom the letters have been sent. Choose one or more, and write a reply in which you provide reassurance and sensible practical advice.

1   I am feeling depressed and trapped by life, mainly because when we go back to school I know I will hate it. This last year at school (I am fifteen and due to take my O levels next summer) has been awful. I have found the work more and more difficult and it got so bad that I began playing truant, taking days off and faking notes from my mother. It is the work that worries me, and my parents expect such a lot from me. I do want to pass my exams. Whom can I talk to, and how can I get over this fear of school?

Julie

2   My friend is rude to me. When I go and call for her she just opens the door and walks back into the living room leaving me to close the door. When inside she sits and reads and hardly says a word to me. Then when I go, I say goodbye and she still sits there reading. I have to see myself out. Why is she being so rude and what can I do?

Alison

3   I'm in a mess and I don't know what to do. You see, when the chance of a school trip abroad first came up my parents said it was not possible. They felt it was a lot of money and that it wasn't fair on my two brothers, who weren't having a holiday at all. But my best friend was going, and so I nagged, and eventually they said I could go if I contributed to the cost. I have a Saturday job in a hairdresser's.

     The balance of the holiday money has to be paid next month and I haven't got it. I should have had the full amount but I'm fifteen pounds short. I know it's my own fault and my parents made it perfectly clear at the time that it was up to me to put the money away regularly, but some weeks I spent money on discos or saw a pair of shoes I wanted.

Now I don't know what to do. I know Dad will be angry and I've been crying myself to sleep in case the whole holiday is cancelled.

Mary

4 I wonder if you could help me. I have a lisp and can't pronounce my s's properly. When I hear myself speak I don't notice it, but I know I have one because I have heard my voice on tape and some of my friends have mentioned it (but not nastily). My mother says she doesn't notice it, but if I'm worried I can go to a speech therapist. I don't want to do that. Is there anything else I can do?

Sally

EXERCISE FOURTEEN

The following lists provide information about two greatly different places.

SOUTHAMPTON – Population 220,000
A city and port in Hampshire – 75 miles south-west of London – on the estuaries of the rivers Test and Itchen – at the head of Southampton Water – facing the Isle of
5 Wight – the city has medieval remains – the Pilgrim Fathers sailed from the port to America – a leading passenger port for America and South Africa – industry includes shipbuilding, cable-making, harbour services, and oil refining – city centre includes new shopping areas
10 and modern stores rebuilt in the 1950s – university – airport – modern sports centre – league football team – county cricket ground   – open spaces, parks and commons within city – frequent ferries to the Isle of Wight – ready access to the cathedral city of Winchester and to
15 the New Forest.

BURY ST EDMUNDS – Population 26,000
A market town in Suffolk – 75 miles north-east of London – 28 miles east of Cambridge – 26 miles from Ipswich and the coast – a historical town – the remains of the abbey
20 include the shrine of St Edmund, King of East Anglia, martyred 870 – now has cathedral – famous market place – old buildings include Guildhall, Town Hall and Shirehall – many fine eighteenth century houses preserved – industries include making agricultural
25 implements and extracting sugar from beet – local shops attract customers from the surrounding rural area which has small beautiful villages – events during the year include Cakes and Ale ceremony in January – commemorates Jenkyn Smyth, the town's benefactor,
30 who died in 1480 – South Suffolk Agricultural Show held in May.

A pen-friend from abroad has the chance to stay with one of two families, one living in Southampton and the other in Bury St Edmunds, and has written to you asking for advice. The aim of the visit is to learn something of the British way of life and history as well as to improve fluency in speaking English.

Bearing in mind the interests that you believe your pen-friend has, write a letter to him or her in reply, pointing out the relative merits of each place and helping with the choice. Use a layout and style appropriate to such a letter. Draw on the details of the two places relevant to your letter; you need not include them all. If necessary, you may supplement the information. *Write the body of your letter in continuous sentences in not more than 200 words.*

EXERCISE FIFTEEN

Below there are three maps drawn by a historical cartographer which set out in graphic form the details and the progress of the Battle of Hastings in 1066:

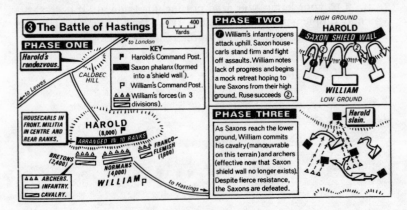

Using only the information given in the maps or their insets, write accounts of the battle as if you were:

a one of King Harold's surviving 'housecarls', *and*

b a Breton soldier fighting in William's army.

Use your own words as far as you can but do not add ideas of your own which you cannot justify from the maps or their insets. *Write in good, clear, accurate English.*

Each of your accounts should not exceed 200 words; *at the end you must state accurately the exact number of words you have used in each.*

EXERCISE SIXTEEN

The following points provide advice on the writing of 'thrillers'.

1   'Thrillers' – which include spy, detective and adventure stories – are read by people who want to escape, for the moment, from the reality of life. The stories must attract interest straightaway and sustain that interest; any improbabilities must be acceptable and unquestioned.

2   'Thrillers' need well-constructed stories, with each chapter ending with a surprise or the creation of suspense.

3   The details of the stories and the background must be carefully planned, and the action must take place in places that seem real to the reader.

4   The hero must be respected, brave, tough and lucky. He must be repeatedly in danger and at least once in the hands of an enemy from whom he escapes.

5   His opponent or opponents must be clever, ruthless, and devious, ready to resort to underhand methods, and, though a match for the hero, attracting no sympathy.

6   The end, where the hero finally emerges victorious, must provide all the answers and tie up any loose ends.

a   A friend of yours is thinking of writing a 'thriller'. Write a letter to him or her suggesting what needs to be kept in mind.

Use an appropriate layout for your letter and restrict the number of words in the body of your letter to not more than 180. The points given above should form the basis for your letter, but you may elaborate, from your own experience of 'thrillers', on what you would want to find.

b   You have been asked to write a review of a 'thriller' for your school or college magazine. Choose a 'thriller' you have enjoyed reading and assess its qualities in the light of the general points made above about 'thrillers'.

EXERCISE SEVENTEEN

Schools and colleges, in both the public and private sectors of education, sometimes issue brochures which are made available to the parents of prospective pupils. Such brochures are intended to persuade such parents that the establishment offers excellent facilities and opportunities to its pupils; some emphasise the advantages of the buildings and the amenities (such as the swimming pool, gymnasium, craft rooms, etc.) or the happy, co-operative atmosphere found everywhere; others emphasise the soundness of the teaching, the smallness of the classes, the examination results, and the qualifications of the staff; and others emphasise relationships with the local community, career opportunities, sporting activities, and subject-emphasis. Often they carry an introductory section which outlines briefly the history of the school or college and summarises the major advantages found there. It selects its material and arranges it persuasively so that the reader will wish to go on to the more detailed pages.

a   Write an introduction *of not more than 200 words* for a brochure designed to introduce parents to your school or college. Decide what approach the brochure will take and write your introduction in *an appropriate style; use good, clear, accurate English. At the end you must state accurately the number of words you have used.*

b   Imagine that you are the Education Correspondent of your local newspaper who contributes a column of about 250 words each week as a special feature; you have decided to write a special article on the local secondary school or sixth-form college, after having received its brochure and after having spent a day visiting the establishment to see it at work. You may wish to match the claims made in the brochure against the facts as you saw them; you may wish to suggest that, whilst there is much to be admired and encouraged, there are features which need radical reform. Above all, you should aim to produce a balanced, objective article which will interest your readers, some of whom will be parents of the pupils themselves, others who disapprove of the establishment, and others who consider that, on balance, it is striving to contribute to the society's welfare.
Select and arrange your material carefully and *write in an appropriate style. Use good, clear, accurate English.* Do not exceed 250 words in length; *at the end you must state accurately the exact number of words you have used.*

EXERCISE EIGHTEEN

The following are notes on a road traffic accident (with personal injury) made by a police constable.

Date: 28 September

Time: 16.08

Place: Junction of Newcome Street and Billingshurst Road

Those involved: Anthony George Hailey (Driver of van, LGH 976; aged 47; motor engineer; Rosa Garage, Billingshurst)

John Arthur Thompson (Driver of taxi NAX 764; aged 32; 37 Endsleigh Road, Billingshurst)

Timothy Paul Richards (Schoolboy cyclist; aged 16; Billingshurst School; home address: 92 Roderick Road, Billingshurst)

Road Conditions: wet after a heavy shower; some oil on the road – result or cause of the accident?

Traffic: moderate to heavy; building up to rush-hour; Billingshurst Road carries the main commuter traffic from Croydon.

Details: 1 Timothy Richards was struck from the right as he was attempting a right turn from Newcome Street by a taxi travelling along Billingshurst Road towards Croydon.

2 After the collision with the boy, the taxi swerved to its offside and collided with a van travelling along Billingshurst Road from Croydon.

3 The boy did not stop at the T-junction; he suffered multiple bruises, a broken leg, and concussion; taken to Billingshurst General

Hospital by ambulance at 16.16. The two drivers were suffering from shock but refused medical help.

4 *Damage:* cycle crushed; taxi extensively damaged on the front and off-side; van extensively damaged on the off-side; one road sign on the central island demolished; van and taxi removed by breakdown vehicles from Rosa Garage at 16.48.

5 Skid marks later showed that the taxi was travelling at approximately 45 m.p.h. before the accident (NB speed limit in Billingshurst Road is 30 m.p.h.). Both drivers have long experience; breath tests proved negative.

6 Traffic was redirected by P.C. Bates of 'S' Division and resumed normal flow at 17.05.

Witnesses: Mrs Jane Wrigley, housewife; aged 54; 33 Drummond Road, Billingshurst; returning from shopping.

Sarah Burrows, schoolgirl; aged 16; returning home on foot from Billingshurst School; 29 Fontwell Avenue, Billingshurst.

P.C. R.G. Smithson, 'S' Division

Give written accounts of the accident and its aftermath for statements made to the police by:

a Mr Hailey, the van-driver;

b Mr Thompson, the taxi-driver;

c Sarah Burrows, the schoolgirl pedestrian;

d Mrs Jane Wrigley, the housewife.

Each account should not be longer than 100 words. Select and arrange your material from the appropriate point of view. Try not to add ideas not suggested by the notes. Write in a style which fits the viewpoint of the person writing the statement; *use good, clear, accurate English.*

At the end of each account you must state the exact number of words you have used.

EXERCISE NINETEEN

The following headlines from different newspapers appeared the first day after an incident at sea when a submarine was lost. In spite of concerted efforts at rescue fifty crew members finally died and later investigations showed that there was an explosion in the engine room which was never satisfactorily explained.

1 SUBMARINE SINKS IN 150 FEET

Cause unknown: explosion feared.
Desperate attempts at rescue.

The Reporter

2 TIME RUNS OUT

Sub. disappears.
3 survivors

Evening Press

3 I WAS TRAPPED

Survivor's undersea ordeal.
64 missing.

The Planet

4 LOST SUBMARINE

Minister orders inquiry
into naval security.

The Informer

a Following a serious accident to a naval warship the Minister of Defence usually makes an early statement to the House of Commons, where a breach of security is not involved, particularly if rumour and speculation are running rife.

Basing your work on the suggestions contained in the above headlines, write a short, factual statement of the kind that a Minister of Defence might make to allay fears and reassure the House that every effort is being made to rescue trapped sailors.

Your statement should not exceed 80 words in length; *write in a style appropriate to the occasion and for the purpose.* Use good, clear accurate English. *At the end you must state the exact number of words you have used.*

b After his rescue on the first day, one of the survivors was interviewed by a news reporter for a television programme. Setting out your work in the form of an interview and maintaining a consistent method of introducing the speakers, write a dialogue that might have taken place between the sailor and the reporter. The purpose of the interview is to present to a national audience at peak-viewing times a vivid account of the sailor's experience from the time the disaster occurred to the moment of rescue. Try to bring out the sailor's attitude (tiredness *or* nervousness *or* relief *or* irritation at the questions) but develop it consistently. The whole conversation should not exceed 200 words in length; *at the end you must state the exact number of words you have used. All the details suggested in the headlines should be included somewhere in the conversation,* but you may also add, in this exercise, a small number of your own ideas suggested by the newspapers. The purpose of this piece of work is to 'slant' material effectively and to use the most effective language for the context specified.

EXERCISE TWENTY

i The first passenger railway in the world was that between
Liverpool and Manchester; it was officially opened on 15
September, 1830. The following is part of a letter written to a
friend by the actress Fanny Kemble who was twenty at the time.
She gives her impressions of a ride on the railway with the engineer
George Stephenson just prior to the official opening.

We were introduced to the little engine which was to drag us along the
rails. She (for they make these curious little fire horses all mares)
consisted of a boiler, a stove, a platform, a bench, and behind the
bench a barrel containing enough water to prevent her being thirsty
5 for fifteen miles, – the whole machine not bigger than a common fire
engine. She goes upon two wheels, which are her feet, and are moved
by bright steel legs called pistons; these are propelled by steam, and in
proportion as more steam is applied to the upper extremities (the hip-
joints, I suppose) of these pistons, the faster they move the wheels;
10 and when it is desirable to diminish the speed, the steam, which unless
suffered to escape would burst the boiler, evaporates through a safety
valve into the air. The reins, bit, and bridle of this wonderful beast, is
a small steel handle, which applies or withdraws the steam from its
legs or pistons, so that a child might manage it. The coals, which are
15 its oats, were under the bench, and there was a small glass tube
affixed to the boiler, with water in it, which indicates by its fullness or
emptiness when the creature wants water, which is immediately
conveyed to it from its reservoirs. There is a chimney to the stove but
as they burn coke there is none of the dreadful black smoke which
20 accompanies the progress of a steam vessel. This snorting little
animal, which I felt rather inclined to pat, was then harnessed to our
carriage, and Mr Stephenson, having taken me on the bench of the
engine with him, we started at about ten miles an hour.
The steam horse, being ill adapted for going up and down hill, the
25 road was kept at a certain level, and appeared sometimes to sink
below the surface of the earth and sometimes to rise above it. Almost
at starting it was cut through the solid rock which formed a wall on
either side of it, about sixty feet high. You can't imagine how strange
it was to be journeying on thus, without any visible cause of progress
30 other than the magical machine, with its flying white breath and
rhythmical, unvarying pace, between these rocky walls, which are
already clothed with moss and ferns and grasses; and when I reflected
that these great masses of stone had been cut asunder to allow our

passage thus far below the surface of the earth, I felt as if no fairy tale
35 was ever half so wonderful as what I saw. Bridges were thrown from
side to side across the top of these cliffs, and the people looking down
upon us from them seemed like pygmies standing in the sky. . .

He (Mr Stephenson) explained to me the whole construction of the
steam engine, and said he could soon make a famous engineer of me,
40 which, considering the wonderful things he has achieved, I dare not
say is impossible. His way of explaining himself is peculiar, but very
striking, and I understood, without difficulty, all that he said to me.
We then rejoined the rest of the party, and the engine having received
its supply of water, the carriage was placed behind it, for it cannot
45 turn, and was set off at its utmost speed, thirty-five miles an hour,
swifter than a bird flies (for they tried the experiment with a snipe).
You cannot conceive what the sensation of cutting the air was; the
motion is as smooth as possible, too. I could either have read or
written; and as it was I stood up, and with my bonnet off 'drank the
50 air before me'. The wind, which was strong, or perhaps the force of
our own thrusting against it absolutely weighed my eyelids down.
When I closed my eyes this sensation of flying was quite delightful,
and strange beyond description; yet strange as it was, I had a perfect
sense of security, and not the slightest fear.
55 At one time, to exhibit the power of the engine, having met another
steam-carriage which was unsupplied with water, Mr Stephenson
caused it to be fastened in front of ours; moreover, a waggon laden with
timber was also chained to us, and thus propelling the idle steam engine
and dragging the loaded waggon, which was beside it, and our own
60 carriage full of people behind, this brave little she-dragon of ours flew
on. Farther on she met three carts, which, being fastened in front of
her, she pushed on before her without the slightest delay or difficulty;
when I add that this pretty little creature can run with equal facility
either backwards or forwards, I believe I have given you an account of
65 all her capacities.

a   Imagine that you were a member of the crowd which watched the
    train passing, seeing it for the first time. You may have been
    standing either beside the track or on one of the bridges high
    above the railway. You were excited by what you saw.

    Write a letter to a friend, giving an impression of what you saw
    and conveying your excitement.

    Your letter should draw on the information provided in the
    passage. The body of your letter should not be more than 200
    words in length.

b Imagine that you are George Stephenson, responsible for the running of the engine and train. Write a report for the directors of the railway company in which you state clearly what the railway engine looks like, how it works, and what it is able to do. Your report should not be more than 160 words long.

c Early railways aroused opposition from some members of the public because of the dirt, disturbance and dangers they created. Imagine that you are a person who objects to the introduction of the railway.

Write a letter to your local newspaper complaining about the building of a railway in your area. In your argument you may draw on details given in the passage, but you should expand on them and slant them to suit the tone of your letter. The body of your letter should not exceed 180 words in length.

ii The following table gives a list of some of the major accomplishments of the British railway system since 1830.

The Best of British Rail

Longest bridge: Tay Bridge	2 miles 364yd.
Bridge with longest span: Forth Bridge	2 spans, each 1,710ft.
Highest railway bridge: Ballochmyle Viaduct (between Glasgow and Carlisle)	164ft. above river bed
Longest tunnel: Severn Tunnel	4 miles 628yd.
Longest straight: Between Selby and Hull	18 miles
Highest altitude: Druimuachdar	1,484ft. above sea level
Lowest point: Severn Tunnel	144ft. below sea level
Steepest mainline gradient: Lickey Incline	1 in 37.7 (nearly 2 miles)
Highest station: Corrour, Inverness-shire	1,327ft.
Station with most platforms: Waterloo	21 platforms
Station with longest platform: Colchester	1,920ft.
Busiest junction: Clapham Junction, over 2000 trains every weekday	
Highest speeds: Advanced Passenger Train	152mph (3/8/75)
High Speed Train	143mph (12/6/73)
Fastest scheduled passenger train: Stevenage-Peterborough, Inter-City 125	Av. 106.25mph
Fastest-ever train journey: *Possible world record* Paddington-Chippenham Inter-City 125	Av. 111.7mph (10/4/79)

The Best of British Rail *(cont.)*

Longest train journey: The Clansman (Euston-Inverness via Birmingham)	568 miles
Heaviest train: Carries iron ore, Port Talbot-Llanwern	3000 tonnes gross
Only BR steam route: Vale of Rheidol Line, Aberystwyth-Devil's Bridge	60cm gauge: 11¾ miles

Making use of all the information provided, write an article in praise of British railways for publication in a magazine which caters for the general reader. Your article, *which should be no more than 200 words in length,* should be written in continuous sentences and correct English with no abbreviations. You are advised to group the information as far as possible.

EXERCISE TWENTY-ONE

A record company is hoping to issue a long-playing record of the best of the Beatles' songs, and you have been asked to write about the Beatles in a 'blurb' to be printed on the sleeve of the record.

Drawing on the information given below, write an article in praise of the Beatles which can be used on the record cover and help in its sales. Your article should be written in continuous sentences and *should not be more than 200 words long*. You may elaborate on the details given, if you wish.

The Beatles

A vocal and instrumental rock 'n' roll group – a major influence on popular music in the 1960s.

Members of the group: John Lennon (born 1940)
                        Paul McCartney (born 1942)
                        George Harrison (born 1943)
                        Ringo Starr (born 1940)

The first three played electric guitars and sang; Ringo Starr played the drums.

All came from Liverpool where they first played in small cellar clubs. They also performed in Hamburg.

1963	Performance at the London Palladium brought them fame. Noticed for their boyish charm, wit, enthusiasm and lack of pretence.
1964	Television performance in America made them internationally known.
	They encouraged British popular music to break away from American domination.
1964	First film *A Hard Day's Night*. Followed by *Help!* and later *The Magical Mystery Tour*.
1965	Awarded MBEs.
1967	*Sergeant Pepper's Lonely Hearts Club Band;* most popular record; sold two and a half million copies in three months. Comment on life in modern industrial society.
1971	Group disbanded.

Wide range of popular songs. Titles include 'Michelle', 'I want to hold your hand', 'Yesterday', 'Eleanor Rigby', 'Lucy in the Sky with Diamonds', 'Yellow Submarine', and 'Penny Lane'.

Experimented with electronic sounds and Indian music. Many lyrics written by John Lennon and Paul McCartney.

Paul McCartney now leads 'Wings', the group which made 'Mull of Kintyre' a best-seller.

EXERCISE TWENTY-TWO

The following is an entry in a dictionary of the world's mammals on the common wolf:

Common Wolf (Canis lupus)

General characters: Large, dog-like with drooping tail. Size variable with region: typical dimensions could be given for male as head and body 4½ feet, tail 16 inches, height at shoulder 31½ inches, weight up to 110 pounds. Bitch is smaller. Typical colour yellowish – or brow-
5 nish-grey brindled with black (Wolves of Arctic tundra often white, on N. American plains generally grey, in Florida often black, but colour phases not completely separated geographically, so black and white wolves may occur in same locality.).

Habits: In pairs or solitary, working over a fixed itinerary, hunting
10 by day, denning up by night in rocky chamber, under roots or trunk of fallen tree, or in holes dug in ground. In summer a family party will remain together, in winter several parties will combine for hunting, well-known howl being used to call members of a party or troop together. Stories of large packs probably refer to troops made up of
15 family parties brought together by hunger.

Habitat: Open country and forests.

Food: Typically large herbivores: e.g. caribou, musk-oxen (in former days, bison), deer, horses.

Breeding: Mating January-March. Gestation 60–63 days. Litters 5–9,
20 young born blind in den among rocks, in burrows or in dense cover. Eyes open 9 days. Weaned 8 weeks.

Present status: Much reduced in numbers. Wiped out over most of Europe except wilder parts of Scandinavia, Germany, France, Spain. N. America, cleared from Eastern States but survive in wilder parts of
25 western USA. Still survive Florida, Mexico.

Range: Europe, Asia (including China, Japan, India, Arabia), N. America.

Longevity: 15 years.

Special comments: Throughout range are numerous local races,
30 differing in size and colour.

Other statistics: Temp. 105° F. (40.5° C.)

Using only the information the entry contains, write an account of the common wolf for:

either **a** inclusion as an article in a popular magazine on wild life;

35 *or* **b** a feature article in *Radio Times* or *TV Times* to introduce a forthcoming TV programme on the life of the common wolf.

Do not add ideas of your own but select and arrange the material contained in the entry as effectively as you can for your purpose. Use
40 your own words and *an appropriate style* and *write in good, clear* English. Whichever approach you adopt, your work should not exceed 220 words in length; *at the end you must state the exact number of words you have used.*

EXERCISE TWENTY-THREE

The following points are taken from a study of shoplifting.

1   Large shops act like a magnet for the shoplifter because there is more there to be stolen and it is apparently less closely checked and supervised.

2   The first line of defence is the shop assistant but, because of expense, stores are tending to use just the bare minimum of staff.

3   Stores make greater use of self-service and self-selection techniques.

4   Shop assistants have uneven periods of pressure. Slack times occur in the early morning before customers start to flock in, and in the afternoon the flow of customers diminishes.

5   At lunch-time the shop fills with customers asking questions and making purchases. The assistant has to move swiftly and may be rushed, becoming tired and irritable. There is also a brief burst of renewed activity just before closing time.

6   At times of bustle and pressure the assistant is too busy to notice people and faces, and just registers the request and the money held out in the extended hand. There is no time to see what other customers are doing.

7   At quiet times lack of awareness as a result of day-dreaming occurs, increased by physical tiredness from standing up for long hours. Only quick unusual movements will catch the attention of assistants.

8   Assistants in large shops are unlikely to be involved in the running and policy of the shops. Their value as individuals making a contribution to the work of the enterprise is not always appreciated.

a   Imagine that you are a security officer for a store. Write a report for the managing director suggesting ways in which you think shoplifting can be reduced. *Use only 150 words.*

b   You are a member of the public troubled by shoplifting. Write a letter to your local newspaper giving reasons why shoplifting occurs and putting forward ways in which it could be reduced.

EXERCISE TWENTY-FOUR

The following extracts form an entry in an encyclopaedia of dates and events for the year 1939.

History

1939 British government's guarantee against foreign aggression to Poland: extended to Greece and Roumania.

Salaries of M.P.s in Britain raised to £600 per annum.

Ministry of Information: war-time ministry in Britain (to 1946).

Lebrun re-elected President of France (to 1940).

Failure of Anglo-French Mission to Moscow.

French Communist Party dissolved for supporting Russo-German Pact.

Barcelona captured by Nationalists under Franco; surrender of Madrid to Nationalists; end of Spanish Civil War.

Mussolini's invasion and conquest of Albania.

† Pope Pius XI; accession of Pius XII.

German unilateral denunciation of Anglo-German naval pact and Polish non-aggression pact.

Salzburg Conference of Rome-Berlin Axis powers.

Czechoslovakia invaded and occupied by Germany (to 1945); Slovakia declared independent state.

Germany annexed Memel.

World War II

Europe: German invasion of Poland, occupation of Danzig: started World War II; Britain and France declared war on Germany; Warsaw surrendered.

Russian Front: Russian invasion of Poland; Fourth Partition of Poland between Germany and Russia; Russian attack on Finland.

Naval: (i) Anglo-German action of River Plate, *Graf Spee* scuttled; (ii) *Rawalpindi*, armed merchant cruiser, sunk by German battleship after gallant action.

Hatay incorporated into Turkey.

Britain and France to assist Turkey in case of aggression.

Esthonia forced into alliance with Russia.

Japanese adopted seceded Chinese leader Wang Ching-wei as puppet ruler in Nanking.

Literature

Joyce Cary (*1888, †1957): *Mister Johnson*, a novel.

Eliot: *The Family Reunion*, a play.

Eric Ambler (*1909): *The Mask of Dimitrios*, a thriller set in the Balkans.

C. S. Forester (*1899): *Captain Hornblower*, a novel; one of a series of tales of a naval officer of bye-gone days.

Isherwood: *Goodbye to Berlin*, stories of life in the city.

Joyce: *Finnegan's Wake*, a novel written in a language unintelligible without concentrated study.

Steinbeck: *The Grapes of Wrath*, American novel.

Flora Thompson (*1877, †1947): *Lark Rise*, a novel.

Gide: *Journal*, diary 1885–1939.

Saint-Exupéry: *Terre des Hommes*, tales of an airman.

Mann: *Lotte in Weimar*, a novel.

Arts

Bartók: *6th String Quartet*, Hungarian work.

Lennox R. F. Berkeley (*1903): *Serenade for Strings*.

Epstein: *Adam*, a sculpture.

Fokine: *Paganini*, ballet for Colonel de Basil.

Hindemith: (i) Violin Concerto; (ii) Violin Sonata in C major.

Honegger: *La Danse des Morts*, Swiss musical composition.

Marin: *Fisherman and Boats*, American painting.

Henry Moore (*1898): (i) *Reclining Figure*, a sculpture; (ii) *Landscape with Figures*, expressionist painting.

Ivor Novello (*1893, †1951): *The Dancing Years*, musical play.

Picasso: *The Poet Jaime Sabartés,* Spanish cubist work.

Piper: *Hamsey Church,* a painting.

Shostakovich: 6th Symphony, Russian composition.

Graham Sutherland (*1903): *Entrance to a Lane,* a painting.

Utrillo: *La Tour Saint Jacques,* French painting.

Films: (i) *Gone with the Wind,* with Vivien Leigh and Clark Gable; (ii) *Ninotschka,* with Greta Garbo.

Excavation of Sutton Hoo burial ship (Anglo-Saxon) in Suffolk.

National Identity Cards introduced into Britain; abolished 1952.

Opening of Opera House, Blackpool; largest in Britain.

Science

Byrd's third expedition to Antarctica (to 1941).

Hans von Chain, of Heinkel's, flew world's first jet aircraft, in Germany.

Halm and Strassman discovered nuclear fission in uranium (U^{235}).

Paul Müller (*1899) synthesized DDT (powerful insecticide commercially produced in 1942).

*born

Igor Sikorsky, of the U.S.A., made first serviceable helicopter.

Balloons used as barrage to protect Britain against aircraft attack.

Radar stations in operation around coast of Britain; proved of great value in giving early warning of aircraft approach.

Morden—East Finchley underground railway, having 17-mile-long tunnel, constructed.

Gloster Aircraft Co. of Britain to build plane suitable for jet engines.

First British transatlantic Air Mail Service opened.

Ministry of Supply established to deal with war-time production; dissolved 1959.

I.F.F. radar (identification, friend or foe) developed.

Excess profits tax in Britain on outbreak of war.

National Service (Conscription) introduced into Britain; to 1960).

White Paper on Civil Defence.

German battleship *Bismarck* launched.

Severe earthquakes in Chile (January) and Anatolia (December); tens of thousands died.

Extermination of anopheles mosquito in Brazil begun (later: Egypt 1944, Cyprus 1946).

†died

Adopt the position of a historian writing today who is interested in *one* of the following fields:

i   political, military, and social history; *or*

ii   the arts and literature; *or*

iii   science.

Using only the information contained in the extracts, write an article from your adopted point of view for inclusion in a textbook to be entitled *The Development of Modern Europe,* in which you try to show that 1939 was a year of special significance in your field.

Do not add ideas of your own; write in an appropriate style and *use good, clear, accurate English.* Your article should not exceed 200 words altogether; *at the end you must state the exact number of words you have used.*

EXERCISE TWENTY-FIVE

The passage in this exercise is taken from an account of the increasingly important part played by women in the world of business, politics, and education.

a Write an article for a women's magazine in which you try to persuade some of your readers to enter higher education. *Use only the information given in the passage* and do not add factual information of your own; direct your writing at the intelligent women amongst your readership, who earlier in their lives missed, for one reason or another, the opportunity to improve their education.

Use an appropriate style and write in good, clear, accurate English. Your article should not be longer than 200 words; *at the end you must state the exact number of words you have used.*

b The first paragraph of the passage suggests that few women have risen to high political rank in the world; the remaining paragraphs give some facts about women's social position and the opportunities they have had or not had in education, and some arguments that have been used to deny women the right to equal educational opportunity.

Write a letter to the editor of *The Times* in which you try, as objectively as possible, to set out some of the reasons why few women have reached 'high positions of political power and influence'.

Use only the information given in the passage; do not add ideas of your own. *Use an appropriate style* and write in good, clear, accurate English. The body of your letter should not be longer than 150 words; *at the end you must state the exact number of words you have used.*

After half a century of women's suffrage, the number of women in high positions of political power and influence is still small enough for them to be known by name. Only three women have (by the mid-1970s) been prime ministers, significantly, all in newly emergent countries (India,
5 Ceylon, and Israel); and although there have been women ministers, some of cabinet rank, in a number of countries, very few have held office outside the spheres that are usually considered women's interests, such as social welfare, public health, and family affairs . . .

Women's vote seems also to bear little relation to their social
10 position in other respects. In France, to give one example, women
have always enjoyed high status not only in the family but also
socially and culturally. The country has produced a number of
eminent women in literature and politics (incidentally, even two
ministers of state in the Popular Front Government of 1936, before
15 Frenchwomen had the vote) and includes among its national heroes a
woman soldier (Joan of Arc). Frenchwomen, nevertheless, were not
enfranchised until 1944.

Switzerland, one of the oldest democracies, did not give women the
vote until 1971. This is all the more curious because not only have
20 Swiss women played a considerable part in the economy of their
country but Switzerland was among the first to extend university
education to women on a basis of complete equality with men . . .

The proportion of women in institutions of higher education is still
considerably lower than that of men almost everywhere. (The term
25 higher education includes teachers' colleges, technological institutes,
and fine-arts colleges, as well as colleges and universities.) . . . There is
a tendency for women students to concentrate in large numbers on a
limited number of subjects – languages, literature, education, usually
social sciences (the list differs somewhat from country to country) – to
30 the near-exclusion of most others. This seems particularly true of the
United States, where as many as 40 percent of women students
graduating in one year (1960–61) qualified in education, another 24
percent in social sciences, including psychology, and 14 percent in
humanities, a substantial proportion of the latter probably also
35 heading for the teaching profession. This leaves very small numbers
graduating in medicine, the natural sciences, the fine arts, law,
engineering, and agriculture. . .

The rationale for denying many a gifted girl equal access with men
to university education is usually that (1) she is not likely to become
40 the breadwinner of a family; (2) her future socioeconomic status will
most probably not depend on her professional occupation or earning
capacity; and (3) her career will presumably be only of short duration,
thus not warranting the investment of time, money, and energy. Some
of these assumptions . . . have been disproved by the facts.

EXERCISE TWENTY-SIX

LUXURY CARPET

You will never see such prices and quality again

> WOOL
>
> THICK PILE
>
> FADE-RESISTANT
>
> HARD-WEARING
>
> BUILT-IN UNDERLAY
>
> CHOICE OF COLOURS
>
> EASILY FITTED

£15.00 (incl. VAT) per square metre

Write to: Dept. AX, FLOORCOVERS Ltd., Hatcham, Lincolnshire, for a quotation (please state measurements accurately)

---

a   Imagine that you followed up this advertisement in a national newspaper and subsequently bought some carpet to cover the whole ground floor of your home. After six months the following defects had appeared:

> some of the pile had become loose;
> patches near the French windows had faded;
> stains did not come out when washed but the dye did;
> the underlay had started to break up;
> parts of the carpet near the door showed signs of wear;
> the carpet had shrunk slightly and pulled away from the skirting-boards.

Write a letter to the managing director of Floorcovers Ltd. of Hatcham, in which you set out your complaints and express your feelings about the quality of the carpet in relation to the advertisement for it.

Use an appropriate style and write in good, clear English. Base your letter on the information given above; *do not add ideas of your own.* The body of your letter should be not more than 175 words in length; *at the end state exactly the number of words you have used.*

b Imagine that you are the managing director of Floorcovers Ltd. of Hatcham, and that you have received a letter of complaint of the kind indicated in **a** above.

Write a tactful reply to the customer. *Use an appropriate style;* write in good, clear, accurate English. The body of your letter should not exceed 150 words; *at the end state accurately the exact number of words you have used.*

a The following map, chart, description and table give information about a package holiday on the Costa Brava in Spain.

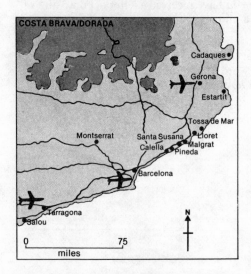

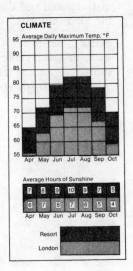

The fine sandy beach is about 600 yards from this large modern hotel which is an ideal choice for a family holiday. The restaurants, bars and cafés in the heart of Salou are only half a mile away and local buses into the resort centre stop just across the road from the hotel.

swimming pool
sun terraces
pleasant garden
spacious bar and lounge
air-conditioning in dining
    room
choice of menu on some
    courses
à la carte menu available
snacks available
TV
Bodega Bar where you can
    dance most nights during
    high season

Airport

You can fly to the Costa Brava from:
    Gatwick 1 hr. 50 mins.
    Luton 1 hr. 55 mins.
    Birmingham 2 hrs.
    Manchester 2 hrs. 10 mins.
    Newcastle 2 hrs. 25 mins.
    Glasgow 2 hrs. 35 mins.

The approximate time for the coach journey to your resort from the airport is: 45 mins.

Hotel Name	HOTEL COSTA BRAVA (Full Board)																		
Jet direct from	Gatwick				Luton				Bristol		Manchester				Leeds		N'cstle	Glasgow	
Nights in hotel	7	10	11	14	7	10	11	14	7	14	7	10	11	14	7	14	14	7	14
Approx take-off time	MON 08.00	FRI 08.00	MON 08.00	MON 08.00	MON 08.15	THUR 23.00	SUN 23.45	MON 08.15	SUN 21.00	SUN 21.00	MON 13.45	TUE 20.45	FRI 20.00	MON 13.45	TUE 14.15	TUE 14.15	TUE 08.00	FRI 08.00	FRI 08.00
Approx home landing	MON 19.15	MON 19.15	FRI 12.45	MON 19.15	MON 13.00	MON 04.30	FRI 03.45	MON 13.00	SUN 20.00	SUN 20.00	MON 12.45	FRI 19.00	TUE 19.45	MON 12.45	TUE 13.15	TUE 13.15	TUE 21.00	FRI 14.15	FRI 14.15
COST IN POUNDS (STERLING)																			
1 May-15 May	103	115	126	147	106	109	118	150	114	158	117	130	134	161	112	156	153	122	166
16 May-22 May	113	127	138	162	116	121	130	165	124	173	127	142	146	176	122	171	168	132	181
23 May-12 Jun	123	137	148	174	126	131	140	177	134	185	137	152	156	188	132	183	180	142	193
13 Jun-26 Jun	133	150	161	184	136	144	153	187	144	195	147	165	169	198	142	193	190	152	203
27 Jun-10 Jul	140	156	167	195	143	150	159	198	151	206	154	171	175	209	149	204	201	159	214
11 Jul-24 Jul	144	161	172	202	147	155	164	205	155	213	158	176	180	216	153	211	208	163	221
25 Jul-11 Aug	150	167	178	209	153	161	170	212	161	220	164	182	186	223	159	218	215	169	228
12 Aug-1 Sep	142	157	168	194	145	151	160	197	153	205	156	172	176	208	151	203	200	161	213
2 Sep-15 Sep	133	148	159	184	136	142	151	187	144	195	147	163	167	198	142	193	190	152	203
16 Sep-30 Sep	123	140	151	174	126	134	143	177	134	185	137	155	159	188	132	183	180	142	193
1 Oct-31 Oct	113	126	–	–	116	120	–	–	124	–	127	–	145	–	122	–	–	132	–
First departure	5 May	2 May	5 May	5 May	5 May	1 May	4 May	5 May	4 May	4 May	5 May	6 May	2 May	5 May	6 May	6 May	6 May	2 May	2 May
Last departure	6 Oct	3 Oct	29 Sep	29 Sep	6 Oct	2 Oct	28 Sep	29 Sep	5 Oct	28 Sep	6 Oct	30 Sep	3 Oct	29 Sep	7 Oct	30 Sep	30 Sep	3 Oct	26 Sep
Flight number	BY027	BY026	BY027	BY027	BY033	BY030	BY031	BY033	BY034	BY034	BY046	BY043	BY044	BY046	BY047	BY047	BY050	BY055	BY055

Departures on or between

All flights weekly.

You are a travel agent who has been asked to provide full advice for

i   a family of four – father, mother, son of sixteen and daughter of eleven – who live in Northampton and want to go to the Costa Brava during the school holidays;

ii a retired couple who live in Brighton and who want the most economical holiday.

Drawing on the range of information provided, write a detailed report for each of these potential clients. Point out what sort of a holiday they can expect, what the travel arrangements could be, and how much such a holiday is likely to cost.

b The following table provides information about a package holiday in Greece.

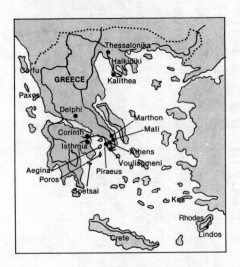

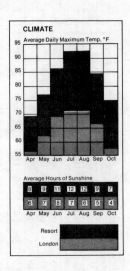

Hotel Name	ATHENS PALACE (Half Board)
Jet direct from	**Gatwick**
Nights in hotel	14
Approx. take-off time	THUR 18.30
Approx. home landing	FRI 01.45
Departures on or between 1 May-15 May	216
16 May-22 May	234
23 May-12 Jun	243
13 Jun-26 Jun	247
27 Jun-10 Jul	252
11 Jul-24 Jul	260
25 Jul-11 Aug	271
12 Aug-1 Sept	265
2 Sep-15 Sept	249
16 Sep-30 Sep	239
1 Oct-31 Oct	232
First departure	8 May
Last departure	9 Oct
Flight number	BY062

All flights fortnightly.

dancing to live music usually once a week
cots and highchairs available for children
children have a section of the main pool
children's playground

The Athens Palace is ideal for a really relaxing holiday. It's set in beautiful gardens just above a long, sandy beach – there's a little funicular railway from the hotel grounds down to the beach, where you'll be able to try sailing and water-skiing. Kalithea village is about one and a half miles away.
colourful, shady garden
terrace areas
separate building with bar and dining room
snacks available
tennis

Airport

You can fly to Athens from:
Gatwick 3 hrs. 35 mins.
Luton 3 hrs. 40 mins.
Bristol 3 hrs. 50 mins.
Birmingham 3 hrs. 50 mins.
East Midlands 3 hrs. 50 mins.
Manchester 4 hrs.
Glasgow 4 hrs. 30 mins.

As a travel agent, you have been asked for advice by a young married couple who live in London on whether they should go to the Costa Brava or to Greece for their summer holiday. Both enjoy sunbathing and like varied entertainment.

Write a report for the couple setting out the information they would need to know and comparing and contrasting the details of a holiday on the Costa Brava or in Greece in June or July. Your report should be written in clear continuous sentences.

c The following paragraph gives a description of a holiday resort typical of a travel brochure.

GRAND BAHAMA

The Bahamas is a country of 700 tropical islands, set in an emerald sea some 50 miles off Florida. A country of palm-fringed beaches, with sand that is either brilliant white or coral pink . . . a land smiled on by the sun, where you can enjoy summer weather all year round. Grand Bahama Island is a kaleidoscope of colourful contrasts, with quiet villages among the lush tropical vegetation only a short distance from the sophisticated sparkle of FREEPORT/LUCAYA, a modern resort with a cosmopolitan air . . . where you can cruise and sail along the superb beachfront, or swim and snorkel over the shallow reefs. Visit too the Underwater Explorers Club, and the Museum of Underwater Exploration in LUCAYA. And at night, FREEPORT/LUCAYA awaits your pleasure with glamorous night-clubs and cabarets – and El Casino, the largest casino in the Western World, opulent in Moorish style. Grand Bahama Island is a shopper's paradise too, with its fascinating International Bazaar in FREEPORT.

Write a 'blurb' or description for a humorous or satirical magazine in which you describe a place you know in a way that makes it most unattractive.

EXERCISE TWENTY-EIGHT

The following are some notes made in Cormack Magistrates' Court on Friday, 20 June, 1979.

Court B	*Date:* 20.6.1979	*Time:* 10.00 a.m.

Accused: John George Dermott, aged 18; apprentice car-fitter. Wendy Jennifer Craig, aged 18; hairdresser.

Charge: Criminal damage. (Breaking street lamp, Cormack High Street; daubing shop fronts with paint.)

Pleas: Not guilty.

Witnesses: Ann Judith Hislop, shopkeeper, Cormack High Street; Andrew William Young, bus-driver, Wentworth Street, Cormack.

Evidence: Dermott and Craig were seen by Ann Hislop in Cormack High Street at 7.30 p.m. on 15.2.1979; both daubed her shop front with paint sprayed from an aerosol can; Craig then, lifted up by Dermott, attempted to remove the bulb from a street lamp above the door of the shop; the glass broke; both accused ran away laughing. Andrew Young, passing by in his bus, observed the incident as related by Mrs Hislop; he reported the matter to Cormack Police Station; both the accused were arrested by P.C. MacTaggart at 7.45 and found in possession of an aerosol paint can; both had traces of paint on their hands and its colour matched that used in the daubings. Dermott and Craig were charged and cautioned, and later released on bail.

Defence: Craig and Dermott saw the paint on the shop front; the lamp was out and they attempted to render a public service by repairing it but the glass broke. They found the aerosol paint can in the gutter in front of the shop just before their arrest.

Verdicts: Dermott – guilty; Craig – guilty.

Sentences: Both were of previous good character; each was fined £10.00 and bound over for twelve months to be of good behaviour.

a Write *two* accounts of the incident as they might have been given by Mrs Hislop and Mr Young to the court. *Each account should not be longer than 75 words.* Use the material given in the above notes and slant it in such a way as to suggest that each speaker was confident that Dermott and Craig were guilty of the offences they were charged with.

b Imagine that the above notes were made by a reporter from a local newspaper that had recently run a campaign against vandalism in the Cormack district. *In not more than 150 words* write a report of the trial as he might have written it for publication in his paper in order to demonstrate his disapproval of the behaviour of Dermott and Craig and to suggest that Mrs Hislop and Mr Young acted as proper, honest citizens in reporting the incident. Use the material in the passage and do not introduce significantly new information in your report.

PART THREE

Summary and Directed Writing

The exercises that follow combine the skills of summarising and directing or 'slanting' the response towards a particular audience. *Read the instructions carefully.* In this Part the material to be used as the basis for the work is to be found in the passages, extracts, tables, forms, diaries or statistics given. No additional information should be added.

EXERCISE TWENTY-NINE

The following extract is taken from *The Diary of Anne Frank*. Anne Frank was a Jewish girl who went into hiding with the rest of her family from the German occupation forces during the 1939–1945 war. They were finally discovered and Anne was sent with her sister to Belsen concentration camp, where she died early in March, 1945, three months before what would have been her sixteenth birthday.

The extract gives an account of a conversation she had with Peter van Daan, the seventeen-year-old son of some Jewish friends with whom Anne and her family went into hiding.

(NB. Anne addresses her diary as 'Kitty'.)

a   Peter did not keep a diary, or if he did, it did not survive the war. Imagine, however, that you were Peter on the evening of Sunday, 19 March, 1944, and that you had decided to begin a diary from that very day. For your first entry give an account of the events that Anne discusses from your own point of view as Peter van Daan.

Use only the information given in Anne's extract. Do not add any details of your own but select what you need from her diary and re-arrange the material as you present it from your point of view as a seventeen-year-old boy in this situation. *Use your own words* and do not copy phrases from the extract or imitate Anne's style of writing. Set your work out in a style appropriate to an entry in a personal diary. Write in good, accurate English.

Your entry should not exceed 200 words in all; *at the end you must state the number of words you have used.*

b   Imagine that you are one of the German soldiers who raided the hiding place on 4 August, 1944, acting on a tip-off from some informers. Before throwing the diary on to a pile of old newspapers (where it was later found by an office cleaner, who handed it to some friends who preserved it until after the war) you flicked through its pages and stopped to read the extract for Sunday, 19 March, 1944. You were both moved and amused by it. Later that night you sat down to write a letter to your wife and children back home in Hamburg.

Give an account of the main details of the entry as if you were writing a paragraph for your letter home. (There is no need to write the rest of the letter; concentrate on the single paragraph summarising the material contained in Anne's entry). *Write in an appropriate style and use good, accurate English.* Your paragraph should not exceed 150 words in length; *at the end you must state accurately the number of words you have used.* Use your own words but *do not add information or details not contained in the extract.*

Sunday, 19 March, 1944

Dear Kitty,
Yesterday was a great day for me. I had decided to talk things out with Peter. Just as we were going to sit down to supper I whispered to him, 'Are you going to do shorthand this evening, Peter?' 'No,' was his reply. 'Then I'd just like to talk to you later!' He agreed. After the
5 washing-up, I stood by the window in his parents' room a while for the look of things, but it wasn't long before I went to Peter. He was standing on the left side of the open window, I went and stood on the right side, and we talked. It was much easier to talk beside the open window in semi-darkness than in bright light, and I believe
10 Peter felt the same.
We told each other so much, so very very much, that I can't repeat it all, but it was lovely; the most wonderful evening I have ever had in the 'Secret Annexe'. I will just tell you briefly the various things we talked about. First we talked about the quarrels and how I regard them quite
15 differently now, and then about the estrangement between us and our parents.
I told Peter about Mummy and Daddy and Margot, and about myself.
At one moment he asked, 'I suppose you always give each other a
20 good-night kiss, don't you?'
'One? Dozens! Why, don't you?'
'No, I have hardly ever kissed anyone.'
'Not even on your birthday?'
'Yes, I have then.'
25 We talked about how we neither of us confide in our parents, and how his parents would have loved to have his confidence, but that he didn't wish it. How I cry my heart out in bed, and he goes up into the loft and swears. How Margot and I have only really just begun to know each other well, but that, even so, we don't tell each other
30 everything, because we are always together. Over every imaginable thing – oh, he was just as I thought!
Then we talked about 1942, how different we were then. We just

don't recognise ourselves as the same people any more. How we simply couldn't bear each other in the beginning. He thought I was
35 much too talkative and unruly, and I soon came to the conclusion that I'd no time for him. I couldn't understand why he didn't flirt with me, but now I'm glad. He also mentioned how much he isolated himself from us all. I said that there was not much difference between my noise and his silence. That I love peace and quiet too, and have
40 nothing for myself alone, except my diary. How glad he is that my parents have children here, and that I'm glad he is here. That I understand his reserve now and his relationship with his parents, and how I would love to be able to help him.

'You always do help me,' he said. 'How?' I asked very surprised. 'By
45 your cheerfulness.' That was certainly the loveliest thing he said. It was wonderful, he must have grown to love me as a friend, and that is enough for the time being. I am so grateful and happy, I just can't find the words. I must apologise, Kitty, that my style is not up to standard today.
50 I have just written down what came into my head. I have the feeling now that Peter and I share a secret. If he looks at me with those eyes that laugh and wink, then it's just as if a little light goes on inside me. I hope it will remain like this and that we may have many, many more glorious times together!

Your grateful, happy Anne.

EXERCISE THIRTY

The following passage is taken from a book by Magnus Pyke on modern food technology and deals with some aspects of factory-farming.

a Write a short speech which might be used as an important contribution to an inter-sixth form debate with another school on the motion 'That this house believes that factory-farming should be developed to feed an ever-increasing world population'. Your speech should support the motion and deal with two aspects of the topic:

    i the efficiency of factory-farming; *and*

    ii some advantages of factory-farming.

Prepare your speech in the form of two paragraphs, one on each of these two topics. Use only some of the information contained in the passage to prepare your speech. Select your material carefully and arrange it in an effective way to persuade your audience to accept your views. *Do not add ideas of your own. Use an appropriate style* and write in good, clear, accurate English.

Your speech should not exceed 175 words altogether; *at the end you must state accurately the exact number of words you have used.*

b Write a second speech which might be used as a contribution to the same debate. This speech should oppose the motion and deal specifically with two aspects of the topic:

    i callousness towards animals in factory-farming; *and*

    ii the misplaced ingenuity of man.

Prepare your speech in two paragraphs, one on each of these topics. Use only some of the material contained in this passage but arrange and 'slant' it to persuade your audience to accept your views. *Do not add ideas of your own. Use an appropriate style* and write in good, clear, accurate English.

Your speech should not exceed 175 words altogether; *at the end you must state accurately the number of words you have used.*

In 1966 W.O. Wilson wrote: 'Poultry production is now conducted mainly in establishments that are best described as factories. A technological revolution has transformed this field of agriculture.' The economic effect of this technological revolution has been
5 profound. In the 1930s few egg farmers kept more than 2,500 hens; in the 1960s 30,000 laying birds were commonplace. In the 1930s the annual consumption of chicken in America was 13.1 lb a head; in the 1960s it was 33.3 lb. And what of the hens themselves? In the 1930s each hen laid on average 121 eggs a year; in the 1960s her successor
10 laid 217.

Chicken farming has been converted from an agricultural operation, often that part of the diverse activities on a mixed family farm considered to be particularly within the area of interest of the farmer's wife, into a manufacturing operation of high technological
15 complexity. The birds, derived from a hatchery providing stock of the appropriate strain, are confined, usually three to a cage, under conditions of controlled temperature, humidity and illumination. Feed, of the exact chemical composition required, is pumped as a slurry round the batteries of cages – or 'nests', as they are sometimes
20 called. The eggs, when they are laid, roll gently into a trough and are carried away on a conveyor belt. They are washed, often oiled to restore the degree of impermeability damaged by the washing, inspected for cracks and defects by candling and conveyed away to be packed. Another conveyor carries out the manure so that the process
25 can be continued for years on end.

Eggs and chicken meat were the first and the most dramatic examples of the evolution of an agricultural process and its metamorphosis into an industrial operation – a part of mainly automated agribusiness. Where the great margarine combines set up
30 plantations of oil palms, the wife of the African peasant could no longer expect to keep as her own the product of his two or three palm trees while her husband supported her and the rest of the family on the other produce of this land. Nor could the wife of the European farmer expect to enjoy, as part of their mutual endeavour, the eggs
35 from a few hens – and an occasional chicken, to boot – when a great supermarket combine had invested a large sum of capital for the intensive production of eggs and standardised, quick-frozen, film-wrapped, oven-ready broilers.

Chickens are clearly only the first of a procession of livestock for
40 which intensive rearing under controlled industrial conditions can appropriately be applied to reduce the cost of labour – which is the same thing as saying, increase productivity – and consequently reduce the price. Pigmeat can be produced along lines quite similar to those used for producing poultry meat. Intensive pig-rearing houses

45 have been elaborated in which a maximum number of animals
   maintained at an appropriately elevated temperature, free from
   disease, will give a high and very economical yield of meat per unit
   weight of feed fed. It has been estimated that one man can handle by
   himself up to 1000 pigs by means of these advanced techniques.
50 Clearly, this is no longer farming. It is agribusiness, an operation
   requiring heavy capital investment and good management that is an
   integral part of food technology.
      The people who were once concerned with raising chickens and
   pigs have for the main found themselves no longer needed for their
55 old work. Comparatively few people, even in pre-industrial times,
   were needed to look after the larger meat animals. Now, dairymen –
   like the dairymaids before them and the milkmen of the future – have
   less and less need to follow their usual pursuits. It can take up to 15
   minutes for a man to milk a high-yielding cow by hand and it is hard
60 work. But whereas one man can therefore only deal with, say, six cows
   if he has to do it by hand, fifty cows are well within his capacity when
   he is equipped with milking machines. And the processes of industrial
   manufacture are being increasingly used, while those traditional to
   farming are being abandoned, in the production of milk as in other
65 aspects of agribusiness based on food technology. For instance, a
   milking parlour may now take the form of a movable production
   line which can be transported from one part of a farm to another; it is
   placed so that the cows can be slotted into their appropriate
   standings, milked by machine and released again to continue eating
70 the grass which it is their function to convert into milk.

EXERCISE THIRTY-ONE

The following statistical tables set out the responses of boys and girls, some of whom left school at sixteen and others who left at seventeen or eighteen, to what schools thought were their main objectives.

a From the viewpoint of *either* a boy *or* a girl **leaving school at the age of sixteen after at least five years in the school,** *using only the information contained in the passage,* set out in *two* paragraphs a summary of the views of your contemporaries (both boys and girls) on what they consider:

i the more important objectives of the school; *and*

ii the less important objectives of the school.

(Remember that you should not limit your statement to the views of your own sex only but try to present in a balanced way the views of both boys and girls, bringing out the differences in their opinions where necessary.)

Your summary should be suitable for publication as an article in a local newspaper interested in the views of the students at its neighbourhood school or college. Select and arrange your material carefully and write in an appropriate style. *Write in good, clear, and accurate English* and *use your own words as far as possible,* although some words and expressions from the original cannot be accurately or economically replaced.

Your finished article should not exceed 225 words altogether; *at the end you must state the exact number of words you have used.*

b Imagine that you are the Headmaster (or Headmistress) writing a letter to the parents of a seventeen-year-old boy *or* girl who has so far spent four years in school. The purpose of the letter is to persuade them that staying on at school a further year will probably lead to a marked change in their son's *or* daughter's views on what the school is trying to do.

Use only the information contained in the tables. *Write in good, clear, and accurate English.* Select your material carefully and arrange it in paragraphs. *Use your own words as far as possible,* although some words and expressions from the original cannot be accurately or economically replaced.

The main body of your letter (i.e. omitting the addresses, and the introductory and final phrases) should not exceed 200 words altogether; *at the end you must state the exact number of words you have used* in the whole letter and how many you have used in the 'main body'.

Percentages saying that various school objectives were very important, by age of leaving school, year at school and sex

School objectives	Age of leaving school	% saying school objective was very important			
		Boys		Girls	
		Year at school		Year at school	
		4th	5th or left school	4th	5th or left school
Help you to become independent and able to stand on your own feet	16	78	71	80	86
	17/18	68	66	80	80
Help you to do as well as possible in examinations like GCE or CSE	16	84	83	85	84
	17/18	88	83	82	86
Help you to develop your personality and character	16	42	36	45	51
	17/18	33	42	44	55
Teach you things which will be of direct use to you in your job	16	76	76	78	69
	17/18	70	66	75	66
Help you to know about what is going on in the world nowadays	16	35	28	36	43
	17/18	23	35	45	39
Teach you plenty of subjects so that you can be interested in a lot of things	16	32	22	44	35
	17/18	26	17	42	47
Teach you things which will help you to get as good a job or career as possible	16	87	90	92	87
	17/18	90	84	85	88
Teach you about what is right and wrong	16	56	54	63	65
	17/18	51	50	56	62

School objectives	Age of leaving school	% saying school objective was very important			
		Boys		Girls	
		Year at school		Year at school	
		4th	5th or left school	4th	5th or left school
Teach you to speak well and easily	16	50	58	72	63
	17/18	55	52	56	57
Teach you to be able to put things in writing easily	16	67	66	69	70
	17/18	68	71	66	68
Do drama in school, that is acting or reading plays	16	7	5	11	12
	17/18	6	5	19	11
Study poetry in school and read or learn poems	16	3	4	5	8
	17/18	4	5	7	7
Teach you things that will be useful in running a home, for example, about bringing up children, home repairs, decorating	16	48	31	58	46
	17/18	24	16	40	30
Teach you how to manage your money when you are earning and about things like rates and income tax	16	77	71	78	74
	17/18	62	54	68	59
Give you sex education	16	33	44	31	48
	17/18	29	31	40	38
Teach you how to behave so that you will be confident and at ease when you leave school	16	53	48	62	68
	17/18	44	50	61	60
Help you to make the most of yourself, for example with your appearance	16	35	33	58	54
	17/18	31	30	35	39

Help you to learn how to get on with other people, for example, those you work with, your future wife or husband	16	56	49	57	58
	17/18	44	35	48	47
Give you interests and hobbies that you can do in your spare time	16	29	21	21	21
	17/18	24	16	21	18
Teach you about different sorts of jobs and careers so that you can decide what you want to do	16	81	76	62	78
	17/18	72	69	80	83
Help you to know what it will be like when you start work, for example, about hours and conditions	16	52	46	48	52
	17/18	33	37	48	40
Take you on visits to factories or offices or other work places to see the different sorts of jobs there are and what the work is like	16	58	59	56	54
	17/18	40	40	39	47
Take you on outings to places like art galleries, the theatre, museums or castles	16	18	22	24	28
	17/18	17	21	24	34
Take you on visits to places like the local fire station or town hall to learn what is going on in the world outside school	16	20	15	19	19
	17/18	14	12	17	11
Run clubs that you can go to out of school hours	16	30	32	24	22
	17/18	30	23	30	26
Take pupils away on holidays	16	27	20	31	26
	17/18	24	29	38	32
Arrange courses in which pupils live away from home for a while	16	35	35	35	34
	17/18	32	29	32	41

EXERCISE THIRTY-TWO

The following passage is taken from an article on television coverage of sport.

a   As a person employed by a television company, write a report for a committee deciding future coverage of sport stating which sports lend themselves to television coverage and which do not and giving reasons why.

Write in correct English and use your own words as far as possible; some words and expressions cannot be accurately or economically replaced but do not copy out long expressions or whole sentences.

Your report should take the form of *a single paragraph not more than 50 words in length.* At the end you should state the number of words you have used.

b   Imagine that you are a sports reporter who believes that television has had a bad effect on sport. Write an article for a television magazine criticizing the televising of sport.

Use only the information given in the passage. Write in correct English and slant the material to suit your particular point of view. Use your own words as far as possible.

Your article should not be more than 90 words long. At the end state the number of words you have used.

c   As a person who enjoys watching sport on television, you are extremely annoyed by the attitude expressed by the sports reporter in his article. Write a letter to the editor of the television magazine conveying your feelings and pointing out what is gained by televising sport.

Use only the information given in the passage; do not add ideas of your own. Use your own words as far as possible, and write in correct English.

The body of your letter should not be more than 90 words in length. At the end you must state the number of words you have used.

With flashbacks, action replays, dramatic against-the-clock finishes and other uses of modern technology, television has worked considerable changes on sport during the past ten years. The most important and emphatic advance may be expressed in a single word 'colour'. Colour was not a new phenomenon in television in itself, but it is only over the last decade that it has been, in Britain, widely diffused, and its diffusion has radically altered the picture and the 'product'.

In the black-and-white past, the accusation against sports television was that it was 'not like the real thing'. In the multicoloured present, the protest has often been that the real thing cannot live up to the television product. The numerous reasons for this vary with the nature of the sport itself. In the case of football, the purist will insist that the television viewer is corrupted by a diet of thrills, of 'edited highlights', of Big Matches and Matches of the Day in which the tedium is pared away to leave only goals, near misses, and penalty box drama. Such a presentation, says the purist, vulgarises the sport.

When it comes, however, to sports with a less panoramic nature, and even (in terms of goalmouth incident) to football itself, it is another story. Who, unless he has a pair of field glasses, can see of cricket what the television camera sees: the ball pitching and breaking, the subtlety of the stroke? Who, unless he has a ringside seat, can possibly see as much of a boxing match as he can see on television? There is golf, too, a sport which has been admirably televised. Colour lends it that pseudo-rural aspect which is part of its evident charm; the trees, the leaves, the fairway, even the bunkers. The camera follows perfectly the arc of the ball, its pitch, its run. Moreover, the cameras can follow several golfers at a time, whereas the best intentioned at a tournament can normally follow only a couple. Many a golfing correspondent has long ago given up the multi-faceted task; he will await his information in the club house.

In these ten years, sports television has perfected above all the instant replay, that standby of the second guesser, that bane of umpires and referees. We take for granted now the immediate small miracle of being shown, a second time and slowly, just what did happen. We take this so much for granted that, after some controversial piece of action at a sports event which we actually attend, we feel slightly irritated that there is no instant replay.

Television, it has often been said, is not an innovator but a parasite. It merely exploits in a lesser medium those talents which have been produced elsewhere such as in the theatre. Even films, perhaps the most popular and diverting form of television, are made less effective by the small screen watched in the commonplace living-room.

So it is with sport – or almost. For television can take sport and turn it into something else. The evaluation of a football match, or any essentially panoramic game, depends on relating the action to what

else is happening on the field or in the arena. One needs a sense of space, which is impossible to gain from a television screen. Yet football really well televised, in colour, with its clever cutting, its judicious
50 zooming, its replays, becomes a marvellous event in itself. No wonder fans have been created without ever going to see an actual game. They miss much of the drama and excitement, but have compensations in comfort and in concentrated action. Tennis particularly adapts splendidly to television. The camera can dwell on the service before
55 widening its view to show what happens to it. It can take in the whole court and the players' movements before zooming in on where a ball lands. It can focus attention on the stars, with their obsessive rituals, contorted faces, and familiar mannerisms.

The list of sports which televise well can be greatly extended: ice-
60 skating, snooker, bowls, show jumping, with the tremulous moment as the pole shakes in its sockets, athletics, too, when important events are being staged. The problem is that television is sometimes inclined to dwarf what it is televising. As the seconds tick away on the screen, while skiers speed downhill or runners race, it seems that basically
65 simple activities have been overshadowed, even ridiculed. These, after all, are sports, in essence child-like, which the immense panoply of modern technology in some sense diminishes.

EXERCISE THIRTY-THREE

The following passage is taken from a book about dinosaurs.

a   Write a definition for an encyclopaedia or general reference book setting out clearly what dinosaurs were like and how they lived.

Use only the information provided in the passage, and write in correct English. Use your own words as far as possible; some words and expressions cannot be accurately or economically replaced but do not copy out long expressions or whole sentences.

Your definition should take the form of *one paragraph not more than 60 words in length.* At the end you should state the number of words you have used.

b   *Using only the information given in the passage,* write an article for a popular magazine criticising the widely-held impression of dinosaurs. You should point out what that impression is and in what ways it is incorrect.

Your article should be written in correct English. Use your own words as far as possible; some words and expressions cannot be accurately or economically replaced but do not copy out long expressions or whole sentences.

Use no more than 140 words. At the end you must state the number of words you have used.

c   You have discovered that many primary school children have a wrong idea of dinosaurs. Prepare the text of a talk to be given by you to a class of eleven-year-olds explaining what dinosaurs were really like.

Use only the information given in the passage; write in correct English. Use your own words as far as possible, and do not copy out long expressions or whole sentences from the passage.

Your text should not be more than 110 words in length. At the end state the number of words you have used.

The word 'dinosaurs' conjures up, for most of us, a hazy picture of the strange prehistoric creatures of the long distant past. Enormous beasts, far larger than any elephant, browse placidly in the steaming

swamps of millions of years ago; while others, less massive but
5 equipped with formidable teeth and claws, stalk their unsuspecting
prey. They have no enemies – except each other – for what lesser
animal would dare to attack such giants?

Nevertheless, in popular legend, the dinosaurs' life of
unchallenged supremacy was far from idyllic; they were beset by
10 problems. We tend to think of them as being cold-blooded, like the
reptiles in the zoo – snakes and alligators, for example – and therefore
not very energetic; they move about very little. When they do move,
they are clumsy and awkward. They trip over tree-trunks, falling and
breaking their legs. Some are so heavy that, once fallen, they cannot
15 even get up again. They have tiny brains and must therefore be
extremely stupid. They need vast amounts of food to keep their
gigantic bodies going; but their tremendous weight and clumsiness,
their slowness and sluggishness and their stupidity appear to give
them little chance of getting it. They cannot run fast enough to catch
20 smaller animals on which to feed and they are not even active enough
to find a sufficiency of plants to eat. Soon they are starving. They die,
one by one, and eventually all are extinct. Only their bones remain.
Now, mounted as skeletons in our museums, they fill us all with
wonder at their fantastic size.
25 This unfortunate story of the dinosaurs and their demise – most of
it wildly incorrect – has resulted in the use of the word 'dinosaur' as a
term of contempt. It is employed to describe something that is
outdated, old-fashioned, perhaps grown too large, too slow and too
cumbersome; something that is no longer much use to itself or to
30 anybody else in our modern world, like the great passenger liners of
the North Atlantic.

The real dinosaur story, however, is very different, and even the
experts do not really know very much about them. Fossil remains of
dinosaurs are still being discovered, and there are lively controversies
35 about their ways of life and the reasons why they became extinct.
Some people seem to think that any large prehistoric animal,
preferably with an unpronounceable name, is a dinosaur, and include
not only the familiar Tyrannosaurus and Brontosaurus but also,
quite wrongly, the winged pterodactyls and the woolly mammoths.
40 Others believe that a dinosaur was one special sort of extinct reptile.
The truth lies somewhere between these two extremes. Dinosaurs are
a special group of prehistoric reptiles, within which there were many
different dinosaurs, just as there are many different mammals today
(hedgehogs, lions, horses, bats, whales, men). Some dinosaurs were
45 very large, weighing eighty tonnes or more – as much as twenty
elephants – but others were quite small; the smallest dinosaur known
was no bigger than a mistle-thrush and could have weighed only a

76

few grammes. Some ran around on their hind legs, but others stayed on all fours. Some ate only plants; others ate meat, killing other
50 animals. One important difference between dinosaurs and mammals was that all dinosaurs lived on land, although some may have ventured into swamps and lakes. None lived in the sea, and none took to the air. They were vertebrate animals, as are we ourselves; they had skull and jaw, backbone, shoulder-bones and hip-bones, and bones
55 of the limbs and feet. Unlike us, they sometimes had a bony armour on the outside as well. Their skeletons suggest that their fore-limbs were nearly always much shorter and more lightly built than their hind limbs. There is no doubt that many could walk on their hind limbs alone, with their heavy tail making it easier for them to raise
60 their front feet off the ground.

Some scientists now believe that dinosaurs were warm-blooded, like birds and mammals. They also believe that the dinosaurs were not all slow and clumsy, that some of them could run very fast and that their legs were suitable for a very active life. Nor is there any
65 reason to suppose that they were any less intelligent than the reptiles of today; it is not so much that their brains were very small, but that their bodies were unusually large in comparison. As a group they existed for a very long time, no other animals competing with them. They must have been highly successful, each well fitted to lead the
70 particular sort of life it had chosen, though today there is nothing but their fossilized remains to show that they ever existed.

EXERCISE THIRTY-FOUR

The following extract is part of a classroom debate on the subject of whether nuclear weapons should be abolished or not. Those taking part are members of a first-year sixth form.

a *Using only the information contained in the extract,* write a summary for a school magazine of:

    i the arguments supporting the abolition of nuclear weapons; *and*

    ii the arguments for retaining and developing nuclear weapons.

Your summary should be in two paragraphs; select the material carefully and arrange it within the appropriate paragraph to make the statement as convincing as possible. *Do not add ideas of your own. Write in good, clear, and accurate English* and use an appropriate style. *Use your own words as far as possible,* but some words and expressions cannot be accurately or economically replaced.

Your finished summary should not exceed 180 words altogether; *at the end you must state the exact number of words you have used.*

b Decide whether you would wish to support the abolition of nuclear weapons or take the side of those arguing for their retention. *Using only the information contained in the extract,* write a speech which might be used in a subsequent resumption of the debate and which exposes the weaknesses in your opponents' case. Do not add ideas of your own but select and arrange the material in such a way that your attitude is supported.

Your speech should consist of not more than two paragraphs. *Use your own words as far as possible,* but some words and expressions from the passage cannot be accurately or economically replaced. *Write in good, clear, and accurate English* and use an appropriate style. Your complete speech should not exceed 200 words; *at the end you must state the exact number of words you have used.*

c Write an editorial for a serious newspaper *either* defending *or* supporting vast national expenditure on research into nuclear arms.

78

Use only the information given in the extract; *do not add ideas of your own.* The purpose of the editorial is to:

  i make clear your newspaper's policy about the matter; and

  ii persuade your readers to adopt your position.

Your editorial should consist of not more than two paragraphs. *Write in good, clear, and accurate English* and use an appropriate style. Your editorial should not exceed 150 words; *at the end you must state the exact number of words you have used.*

(The success of your editorial will depend on your selection and arrangement of material as well as on its presentation. *Use your own words as far as possible,* but some words and expressions cannot be accurately or economically replaced.)

Mark: It's up to us as young people to see that the earth we have to live on isn't spoilt. Nuclear weapons are quite different from all the other weapons used in the past; once they explode they contaminate vast areas with radioactivity
5   and this radioactivity lasts for years and years.

Elizabeth: I think it's a good job we have them. The fact that they exist helps to stop wars – or, rather, makes them much more unlikely ever to start. No civilised country would deliberately make half the world uninhabitable and risk
10   having its own land destroyed. If one side used an atom bomb the other one would soon retaliate.

Janet: Yes, but what about those who cannot retaliate? The 'civilised' nations, as you call them, stopped using poison gas on each other merely because they were afraid of
15   retaliation but the Italians still used it on the Abyssinians in 1936. They knew the Abyssinians couldn't use it in return because they did not have it. In any case, once an atom bomb has fallen on your head you are unlikely to be able to send one back.

20 *Elizabeth*: There will always be someone left to fight back but I still maintain that major wars can be avoided merely because these weapons exist. Take the Cuban crisis in 1962, for instance. Neither the Americans nor the Russians were willing to risk an all-out nuclear war and so they found a
25   peaceful solution to their argument.

Paul: There's one argument in favour of developing nuclear bombs that nobody has mentioned so far. The scientific research necessary to make them often has advantages for our daily lives. We need nuclear energy to provide us with
30 energy once the world's oil supplies run out. How are we going to run our factories and heat our houses without it in the year 2000?

Janet: Oh, you can't justify research into killing millions of people by saying that it might have some useful spin-offs.
35 If you want to use nuclear energy for peaceful purposes, why not spend all your research resources on developing *that*?

Mark: I agree with Janet, here. We spend too much of our nation's resources in making weapons, that soon become
40 obsolete anyway, to destroy men, women, and children. Think what we could do with all the money saved, if we spent it on hospitals, schools, and the old!

Paul: That's no argument; what you've just said would apply just as well to expenditure on any form of defence. If we
45 fought with bows and arrows and then decided to abolish war we could spend the money saved on these weapons to make the world a better place.

Elizabeth: We've not managed to abolish war yet and until we do it makes sense to defend ourselves with the best weapons we
50 can invent. In any case, it's just as immoral, if we take Mark's argument seriously, to kill men, women, and children with bows and arrows as kill them with atom bombs.

Mark: That's not what I said, and Elizabeth knows it. But it is
55 more immoral to condemn vast generations yet unborn to the risk of cancer caused by radioactivity than to kill a few hundred of the enemy.

Paul: Why? I see, it's all right to kill one man but not all right to kill thousands! If killing is wrong, it's just as bad in
60 principle to kill one person as to kill several.

Janet: You could argue that to use a few atom bombs in a war might shorten the fighting and actually save lives that would otherwise be lost. When the atom bombs were dropped on Hiroshima and Nagasaki in the last war, the
65 fighting stopped almost at once. Thousands of lives were

80

saved that might have been lost if the Japanese mainland had been invaded by conventional forces.

Mark: Whose side are you on?

Janet: I'm on the side of mankind. My whole future depends on
70 an answer being found to this problem. Obviously I'd prefer the country's wealth being spent on hospitals, power, research into disease, and making the deserts provide food for the starving millions, but if we abandon nuclear weapons we may be overrun by others and have
75 no life at all.

Mark: My fear is that if we have nuclear weapons one day we'll use them and then the world's green fields will be turned into deserts.

EXERCISE THIRTY-FIVE

The following passage and lists are taken from a comparative study of small retailing outlets.

a   *Using only the information given in the passage and lists,* write an account for a colour magazine supplement of the major changes which took place between 1853 and 1958 in the stock of the small general shop. Avoid giving long lists of goods but look for ways of grouping them in order to bring out significant changes. Use an appropriate style and *write in good, clear, accurate English. Use your own words as far as possible,* but some names and expressions cannot be accurately or economically replaced. (In this exercise do not generalise details to such an extent that meaning is lost, but do not merely repeat at length lists of unnecessary names.)

Your account should not exceed 200 words altogether; *at the end you must state the exact number of words you have used.*

b   Imagine that you are a young manager in your twenties of a retail shop today. Write a letter to your aged grandfather setting out for him some of the major changes that have occurred in retailing since 1958.

Use only the information and evidence given in the passage and the lists. Do not add ideas or details of your own. Write in an appropriate style and make the letter clear and coherent. *Use good, accurate English* and set out your work in an acceptable and consistent letter form. *Use your own words as far as possible* but obviously you will have to draw on names and expressions from the original passage and lists to make your points.

The main body of your letter (i.e. not counting the address, introductory phrases and initial paragraph of greeting as well as the concluding farewell and signature) should not exceed 200 words altogether; *at the end you must state the exact number of words you have used* in the whole letter and how many you have used in the 'main body'.

c   Make a list of some of the more important inferences which can be drawn from the information given of changes that have taken place in:

    i   the shopping habits and diets of families from 1853 to 1980; *and* our everyday living brought about by inventions and developments in travel, hygiene, and nutrition as well as marketing since 1853.

Using the information you have drawn from the evidence *and no other* write a factual statement *in two paragraphs* of changes corresponding to **i** and **ii** for a magazine directed at the general reader.

Write in good, clear, accurate English and use an appropriate style. Use your own words as far as possible. You should not use more than 200 words altogether for your two paragraphs; *at the end you must state the exact number of words you have used in them.*

Among pure retailers, the role of the very general shop is obviously predominant in all these and many other examples. Something of the flavour of a village general shop may be gained from a recommended inventory for country shopkeepers which appeared in a handbook for retailers published in 1853. This, so obviously not an exhaustive list, at least suggests a marked advance on the dreary, amateurish village shops of a century before. It makes an interesting comparison with the inventory of a present-day small general shop.

The author of this nineteenth-century guide, who was preaching the need for up-to-date methods and good service, advocated making up many of these goods only on demand, so that they would be sold fresh, but to save keeping the customer waiting longer than was absolutely necessary, he suggests that wrapping-paper may be conveniently kept ready—cut to handy sizes. Verdigris on the scales and pans is a bad thing, as it has been known to contaminate food, and polishing the counter with the apron may give an untidy appearance, while 'such filthy practices as chewing a cork before use or blowing into a bottle to remove dust, *must* be abstained from'.

STOCK OF THE SMALL GENERAL SHOP, THEN AND NOW

1853	1958
Grocery. Tea, coffee, cocoa, chocolate, chicory, spices, barley, patent flour, semolina, sauces, pepper, mustard, birdseed, scent.	*Foodstuffs.* Butter, margarine and other fats, cheese, sugar, cakes, sweets, chocolate, biscuits, rice, sago, tapioca and similar goods, bacon, cooked

Chandlery. Black-lead, paste-blacking, starch, grits (prepared), night-lights, German paste, twine, cord, rottenstone, emery, whiting, putty-powder, oxalic acid, sweet-oil, soda, sandpaper, bath-brick, Fullers' earth, congreve matches, soap, blue, gum, etc.

Hardware. Nails, tools, cutlery, tinware, toys, turnery (i.e. brushes, clothes pegs and other cheap wooden items), garden seeds, stationery.

Drapery. Cheap cotton and woollen piece-goods, needles, threads, wool, beads, etc.

Drugs. (To be compounded by the shopkeeper) purgatives (black-draughts from senna, ginger, etc.), siedlitz powders, adhesive plaster, ginger beer (stone bottles from the Potteries at 10s. a gross), soda-water powders, sherbert powders, ginger-beer powders, baldness pomades, tooth-powders, hair-dyes, phosphorus paste for rats, inks, bug-poison.

from *The Shopkeeper's Guide* (Anon.), 1863

ham, breakfast foods such as cereals (all the popular ones), oatmeal and porridge oats, rusks, flour, bread, teacakes or muffins (occasionally), currants, sultanas, raisins, dates, figs, glacé cherries, candied peel and other dried fruits, eggs, jams, frozen food and vegetables, custard powders, blancmange, jellies, fish and meat paste, etc.

Tinned foods. Meat, fish, peas, carrots, fruit of all kinds, syrup, Russian salad, sandwich spread and similar goods, tinned milk and vegetables for babies, tinned skim milk, full cream condensed milk, soup (also in packets).

Spices and Flavourings. Salad cream, salt, pepper, mustard, vinegar (bottled and loose), mixed spice, ground almonds, vanilla and other essences or flavourings, sauces (horse-rad-ish, tomato, etc.), pickles, pickled cabbage, chutney, Marmite.

Drinks. Tinned ground coffee, proprietary brands of coffee compound, liquid coffee extract, tea, cocoa, drinking chocolate, mineral waters, fruit squashes, Lucozade, syphons of soda water, Bovril, Oxo.

Greengrocery. Potatoes, carrots, cabbages, tomatoes, other vegetables in season (peas, beans, cauliflower, etc.), oranges, lemons, apples, salad greens.

Hardware. Scrubbing brushes, clothes lines and pegs, fly and insect sprays, pan-cleaners, steel wool or similar, toilet rolls, firelighters.

Fancy goods. Pins, needles, knitting needles, cotton, some silks, darning wool, silk, rayon and ladies' nylon stockings, children's socks, birthday cards, doylies, cake-cases, writing paper and envelopes, buttons, hair-nets, combs, hairpins.

Cleaning materials. Soap (washing and toilet) soap powders and grease-solvents, shampoos, synthetic detergents in bewildering variety, disinfectants, W.C. cleaner, shoe-polish, floor-polish, dyes, window cleaning materials, Brasso, Silvo.

Toilet requisites. Shaving soap, face cream, powder (baby, talcum and face), lipstick, hand cream and certain other cosmetics, brilliantine hair cream, setting lotion, health salts of various kinds, cough medicine, toothpaste, aspirin, baby's comforter, cotton wool, sanitary towels, liniment, olive oil.

Other goods. Cigarettes, pipe tobacco, matches, small cigars, drawing pins, stamps, electric light bulbs, drinking straws, ice-cream, lollies.

from W. Burns, *British Shopping Centres,* 1959

1980

Presentation. Self-service. The goods should be displayed in a manner likely to attract customers: promotional lines at eye-level; common groceries for the weekly shopping basket at different points throughout the store to encourage movement; shelves to be kept well-filled; cheap or reduced lines to be clearly ticketed; floors free of boxes and obstructions; easy and swift access to the check-out; packaging should be used to conserve space and produce rapid turnover.

Food. Butter, margarine, yoghurt, cream, fresh and long-life milk, eggs. Delicatessen: fresh-cut ham, salami, pâtés, bacon, pies, sausages. Cheese: Danish blue, Gorgonzola, Stilton, Edam, Wensleydale, Derby, English and Canadian cheddar; Austrian smoked; German smoked with ham; pasteurised processed. Spices: salt, pepper, pickles, salad cream, sauces, ketchup, curry powder, relishes.
Rice, tapioca, semolina. Dried fruit: currants, sultanas, raisins, apricots, figs. Jams and preserves: jellies, tinned fruit; tinned milk,

syrups, meats, vegetables; spices (drums and small packs). Packed biscuits. Baby foods.

Flour, bread, rolls, crumpets, crispbreads, French toasts, cornflakes, Shredded Wheat, and other cereals; sugar, castor, granulated, cube, demerara, brown; treacle and syrup; honey. Chocolates and sweets – placed near checkpoint exit.

Drinks. Tea (arranged by brand). Coffee: instant, beans (prepacked), ground, with chicory. Lemonade, squashes, mixer drinks, Shandy. Cocoa, drinking chocolate, Horlicks, Ovaltine, Lucozade.

Frozen foods. Cabinets to be kept shut but clearly marked on the lids with special offers, etc. Meats; fish, fishcakes and fish fingers; seafoods; cakes; pastry; whole meals; ice-creams and sorbets; deserts and fruits; pies. Poultry. Rabbits.

Greengrocery. Prepacked tomatoes, lettuce, cabbage (red and white), leeks, carrots, onions, potatoes, oranges, lemons, apples (English, French and S. African), grapes; fennel, aubergines, green and red peppers, yams, sweet potatoes; avocado pears; soft fruits (in season); potted plants.

Household and other goods. Napkins, toilet rolls, aluminium foil, cling foil, plastic bags; toiletries, razor blades, tights, aerosols; washing powder (including automatic and bio), soaps (household and toilet), dishwasher powders and rinses; brushes, mops, dishcloths, paper rolls, carpet cleaners, floor and shoe polishes; combs, firelighters, matches. Toothpaste; bathcleaners, toilet cleaners.

EXERCISE THIRTY-SIX

The following passage is taken from a study of child chimney-sweeps in the nineteenth century.

a   Using only the information given in the passage, make a summary, for an article in a historical magazine, consisting of *two* paragraphs:

i   the conditions which child sweeps endured; *and*

ii   the reasons why their employers and the public continued to use child sweeps.

Do not try to summarise everything in the passage, but select from it the material needed for your paragraphs. *These should be written in an appropriate style and in clear and correct English.* Some words and expressions cannot be accurately or economically replaced, but do not copy out long expressions or whole sentences; *use your own words as far as possible.*

Your complete work should not exceed 150 words altogether; at the end you must state the exact number of words you have used.

b   Write an account to present to a government official inquiring in 1840 into the conditions in which child sweeps work to persuade him that urgent reform is necessary. You may write from the point of view of *either* **i** a local religious leader *or* **ii** the parent of children who are fortunate not to have to work at chimney-sweeping *or* **iii** the parent of a child who works as a chimney sweep. (Make it clear which of the three approaches you are adopting.)

Write in clear and correct English and use a style appropriate to a persuasive account. *Use only the information given in the passage* as a basis for your work. Select the relevant material and arrange it carefully before you begin to write your account, *which should not exceed 100 words in length; at the end you must state the exact number of words you have used.*

c   Write a letter to an important national newspaper from the point of view of an employer of young chimney-sweeps in 1840, in which you present your reasons, as objectively as you can, for continuing to use boys in this occupation. The purpose of the letter is to convince the readers that a reform of the law was not only unnecessary but undesirable.

Write in clear and correct English and use an appropriate letter form. *Use only the information given in the passage* as a basis for your work. Select the relevant material and arrange it carefully before beginning to write your letter, *which should not exceed 100 words in length; at the end you must state the exact number of words you have used.*

In 1840 an Act had been placed on the Statute Book forbidding the climbing of chimneys by children, and yet in the eighteen-sixties the employment of boys for the purpose was actually increasing. Year after year children were bought and sold to a life of dirt and suffering,
5 ended for many of them by a revolting form of cancer due directly to their occupation; year after year a child or two from the miserable number reached local notoriety by being suffocated in a flue; year after year persons otherwise kindly and humane continued to have their chimneys swept by children.
10   It is a strange story, and if we ask the reason why the practice continued, the answer must be sought in some curious attitude connected with the Englishman's love of his home and dislike of interference. The Englishman's home is his castle, and to dictate the method in which his chimney should, or should not, be swept, a
15 dictation which might even involve an alteration in that chimney, meant an interference with private affairs. And the more closely his home resembled a castle, and the more chimneys he possessed, the more vehement became his opposition to interference. Thus it happened that the House of Lords were long the champions of
20 domestic privacy, protecting what they called the 'rights of property'. The arguments by which they resisted reform were often ludicrous in character, but they were reinforced in practice by a solid mass of housewifely prejudice, deaf to all appeal, convinced that soot would be scattered and furniture injured if machinery were used in place of
25 boys.
    Appeals to the conscience of the housewife actually had the effect of encouraging the employment of boys, for uneasy feelings about the 'dear little boys' prompted presents of coppers and food, with the result that, as the children received more money than would keep
30 them in clothes, and more food than they could eat, they were more profitable to their masters than a machine, which cost money to buy and was not rewarded with coppers or scraps of food.
    The evidence given by sixty-three witnesses before a Commission in 1862 was enough to shake the confidence of the firmest believer in
35 'the moral feelings of perhaps the most moral people on the face of the earth'. There were tales to show that a child's tender flesh had to

be hardened for the work by rubbing with brine. At first children would come back from their work with their arms and knees streaming with blood, and the knees looking as if the caps had been
40 pulled off. Then they had to be rubbed with brine and perhaps go off to another chimney. There was the same forcing of terrified children up the dark narrow flues; one master sweep remarked that a bit of mortar no bigger than an egg, or even smaller, might fix you tightly wedged in the chimney. All children 'want a deal of coaxing or
45 driving at first', and 'if, as often happens, a boy is gloomy or sleepy, you must ill-treat him somehow, either with the hand or brush or something'.

EXERCISE THIRTY-SEVEN

The following passage is taken from a book which discusses schooling during the Second World War.

a Write a summary as if by a government official for his Head of Department, reporting on the effects of war conditions on children's schooling.

Using only the information given in the passage, give a clear factual account of what happened and the effects.

Write in correct English and use your own words as far as possible; some words or expressions cannot be accurately or economically replaced, but do not copy out long expressions or whole sentences.

Your summary should be *a single paragraph not more than 120 words in length. At the end you must state the number of words you have used.*

b Imagine that you were at school during the war, and that your children have now expressed sympathy for you because of what you and other children had to face at that time.

Write an account for your children of what school life was like at the time, showing that their sympathy is not really necessary.

Use only the information given in the passage; do not add ideas of your own. Write in correct English and use your own words as far as possible.

Your account should be not more than 120 words in length. State at the end the number of words you have used.

For most children the war was an interesting time to be at school, or, all too frequently, to be away from it. The government, having evacuated their pupils, had intended to keep the schools in danger areas closed for the duration of the war, and it was not until two
5 months after the beginning of the war that, very unwillingly, a few were reopened; many could not be, as they were now Civil Defence depots or fire stations. By February 1940 nearly a third of all children in the cities were receiving no education at all. More schools reopened in September 1940, just in time for the blitz. By July 1941
10 1000 of the 23000 state schools in England and Wales had been

wholly or partly destroyed, and 3000 more damaged. Most schools were fortunately hit at night, but due to the strain of broken nights and interrupted travel school attendance again dropped sharply. Family difficulties swelled the total, for where the mother had a war 15 job, older children often had to stay at home to care for the babies or take her place in the queues at shops. For the first time for a generation, too, lack of footwear – due now to the war, not to poverty – became a major cause of absence from school.

For most teachers, the outstanding feature of the war was not the 20 empty desk, but the crowded classroom. Twenty thousand male teachers had been called up and some women teachers had been transferred to other duties, like running rest centres. With too many pupils, too few books, too little equipment – some classes even had to share pencils – teachers did heroic work, but, for the first time since 25 education had become compulsory in 1870, education standards dropped. By 1943 the London County Council inspectors were finding that twice as many children aged thirteen to fourteen could not manage a simple reading book as twenty years before and that the number of misspellings in a simple composition had doubled.

30 In evacuated areas 'home schools' were common, with from eight to a dozen children meeting one or two mornings a week in a private house. An Enfield boy remembers his as involving mainly games with 'a bit of writing and reading'. Many wartime memories of school centre on long hours spent in the shelters. A Sussex girl, seven in 35 1939, observed 'no panic, just a feeling of excitement as each class marched quickly across the playground to the shelter... Each child had a tin or box in which to keep comics, a book, some sweets and a favourite toy to be occupied during the raid.' For most children, raids were a not unwelcome interruption to the day's routine. Sometimes 40 parents had the option of allowing their children to remain on the school premises or at their own risk dash home.

It was interesting to note the difference between the dash for home and the time taken to cover the same distance back to school after the All Clear. Alerts at night were equally popular, for if the siren 45 sounded before midnight morning school was postponed for one hour, and invariably 'children reproved for arriving at the later hour were certain that it was before midnight by their clock that they were awakened'.

For those with no liking or aptitude for games the war was also a 50 great liberator. Even at schools which had compulsory games or military training every single day, except Sunday, it was at last possible to escape occasionally from the humiliation, boredom and time-wasting of the cricket or rugger pitch to work for a local farmer, for which one was even paid. Shortages of sports equipment, from

55 hockey balls to gym shoes, also protected some children from the
normal team-game tyranny. Girls in one school which had lost its
tennis courts and netball pitch to the Army were reduced to playing
table-tennis, while in a Walthamstow school first aid classes replaced
physical training.

60　On the whole lessons were less affected than out-of-school activities. Wartime chemistry lessons included instruction in water
purification on which the sixth-formers would have been employed
if bombs had breached the water-mains, but due to the shortage of
equipment most experiments had to be taken on trust. In girls' schools
65 the war made itself felt most in domestic science lessons, now more
essential than ever, for many mothers were afraid to let their
daughters experiment on scarce rations or clothing at home. Even
laundry lessons were planned to avoid waste of soap and hot water.

One wartime change was destined to become permanent: the
70 provision of a midday meal at school, free for the poorest children,
fourpence halfpenny for the rest. 'Dinner duty' became yet another
chore for the harassed teacher to crowd into the day and, at least in
the beginning, the food was often poor. One unusual task placed upon
head teachers was deciding which children were growing at more
`75 than the normal rate and thus entitled to additional clothing
coupons. Adaptability and resourcefulness had always been in
demand in the teaching profession, and the war years showed these at
their best.

EXERCISE THIRTY-EIGHT

The following is taken from a discussion by sixteen-year-olds about old age.

a *Using only the information provided,* write a summary setting out the attitude of old people to the young and to the world in which they live.

Write in correct English and use your own words as far as possible; some words and expressions cannot be accurately or economically replaced but do not copy out long expressions or whole sentences.

Your summary should take the form of *a single paragraph not more than 75 words in length. At the end you must state the number of words you have used.*

b The discussion contains views sympathetic towards old people and, by contrast, intolerant of them. Prepare *the texts of two speeches* to be given in a school or college debate, *the first favourably disposed towards old people,* and *the second critical of them.*

Use only the information given in the passage; do not add ideas of your own. Write in correct English and slant the ideas to suit the particular point of view. Use your own words as far as possible.

Devote a paragraph to each speech. *Your two paragraphs should not exceed 140 words in total,* though they need not be evenly balanced. *State at the end the number of words you have used.*

Robin: When you read about old people in the papers or see programmes about them on television, they are always shown as sad and ill or lonely. There they are, the people who worked for a little wage and who are being dumped.

5 Pat: It certainly is very hard to imagine now what any of us will be later. I remember asking my grandfather about this and he said that you never think of yourself as old. He thought of himself as being a young boy of about twenty-two when he was in his *seventies*.

10 *Linda*:   What I will hate will be the changed appearance. Everybody will see it and think, 'That is an old person.' I wouldn't want to be classed as an old person.

Robin: I see them merely as people.

Colin: I don't think the old want to be us. Society changes and they
15 don't envy our society any more than we envy theirs. Old people seem to want what they have had, not what the young have got.

Robin: Do we talk naturally to the old?

Graham: I talk naturally. My grandparents like to know what I am
20 doing, where I'm going, whereas my parents are more interested in how I'm getting on.

Sarah: I'm like Graham. I never adapt my conversation.

Victor: Our grandparents certainly seem to have enjoyed the Second World War. They always cheer up when it is
25 mentioned. They are very proud about how they endured its hardships. I've always felt that the war was the turning-point in their lives. It sort of trapped them somewhere between the old ways and the new.

Tim: Our education is carrying us further away from them. My
30 grandparents are proud that I have got to this school, but I don't know that it is causing any separation. My grand-father is a miner but I know he sees himself in me. He has a huge understanding of things and an acceptance. I think what separates us from him is our freedom. He worked as a
35 little boy. At fourteen he was a full-time worker. How can I understand what any of that means? A lot of old people call the young unprincipled just because we can't understand their working childhoods. My grandparents will stare at me physically, they'll watch how much I eat or listen to the
40 way I talk, and nod to each other. I can see that I am very interesting to them.

Graham: I think that old people like young people around. It's easier to talk to my grandparents than it is to my parents. They understand what I am talking about.

45 *Gillian*:   My grandmother is blind and she can't hear, and her life is absolute misery. I would advocate euthanasia for her situation, as cruel as it may seem.

Linda:	I agree. There are so many old people now. Everybody is staying alive too long. It sounds cruel, but I think that after about the age of seventy there should be euthanasia. It is a shame that so many old people are kept alive. They waste the tax-payer's money and fill up the geriatric wards.
Pat:	At *seventy*? One of my aunties is seventy and she's just incredible. Lots of relations on my father's side have been pensioned-off but they're certainly no burden at all.
Colin:	My gran is seventy-five and she still goes dancing twice a week.
Robin:	You can't look on the old as a separate entity. They are human beings and have as much right to pleasure and food and friends as we have. Pushing out the old is savage.
Peter:	How frightened you are of the old!

EXERCISE THIRTY-NINE

The following passage is taken from a book which discusses man's relationship with the animals which share the world with him and which are threatened by him.

a   Prepare a *factual* introduction, of the kind a chairman might give, to a discussion at a school debating society on the extinction of the world's wild life. *In a single paragraph* set out:

> the factors which *directly* contribute to the extinction of certain living creatures.

Use only the information given in the passage; select and arrange your material so that the relevant facts are given clearly and accurately. *Write in correct English and use a style which is appropriate to what you are doing. Use your own words as far as possible*; some words and expressions cannot be accurately or economically replaced but do not copy out long expressions or whole sentences.

Your finished paragraph should not exceed 175 words altogether; *at the end you must state the exact number of words you have used.*

b   Prepare a contribution to a school debate on the subject of the extinction of the world's wild life. Try to *persuade* your audience that the real threat comes from:

> the *indirect* factors which contribute to the danger.

Use only the information given in the passage; do not add ideas of your own. *Write in correct English and in a style which is likely to persuade* your audience to accept your arguments. *Use your own words as far as possible*; some words and expressions cannot be accurately or economically replaced but do not copy out long expressions or whole sentences.

Your finished paragraph should not exceed 175 words in length; *at the end you must state the exact number of words you have used.*

c   The passage implicitly condemns man for his actions which lead directly and indirectly to the extinction of many forms of wild life. *In a single paragraph* set out the arguments which man might use to justify his actions.

Use only the information given in the passage; do not add ideas of your own. *Write in correct English and try to present the arguments as clearly and as dispassionately as you can. Use your own words as far as possible*; some words and expressions cannot be accurately or economically replaced but do not copy out long expressions or whole sentences.

Your finished paragraph should not exceed 150 words in length; *at the end you must state the exact number of words you have used.*

Man directly brings about the extinction of an animal when he sets out to kill it in large numbers and is heedless or ignorant of the fact that the species cannot reproduce itself fast enough to make good the losses; he is indirectly responsible for the extinction of animals when he alters
5 their natural environment for his own purposes to such an extent that they cannot survive.

Animals have always provided man with an important source of his food supply. So long as he hunted with primitive weapons he could not threaten any species; the Indians had hunted the American buffalo
10 herds for thousands of years but the building of a communication system in the form of the Union Pacific Railway led to special hunting parties to supply meat for the construction workers. It was not long before the hunting for food developed into hunting for sport; the buffalo were shot with high-powered, accurate rifles and by 1890 only
15 a few dozen buffalo remained. Man felt some justification, however, for killing animals in large numbers when he thought they competed with him for his food supply; the Tasmanian wolf looked a little like a kangaroo and wrongly attracted the reputation of stealing man's food with the result that it was completely exterminated. Likewise the
20 Carolina parakeet was eliminated by angry farmers for attacking their fruit.

The fate of the passenger pigeon was similarly unhappy: its savoury flesh, its migration in dense flocks, and its habit of nesting in swarms were sufficient to ensure its total downfall. The destruction of forests
25 to make new routes and settlements and to provide agricultural land also wreaked havoc. The soil was depleted by intensive use and the land turned into a gigantic dustbowl. The wild turkey and the heath hen, as well as the wapiti and the white-tailed deer, once plentiful in the former forests of the eastern United States, all had to struggle to survive. The
30 forest cougar, too, which preyed on these forest animals died out with its source of food.

In order to cultivate land man developed powerful herbicides to destroy vegetation and effective chemical fertilizers to increase his

crops. Unfortunately they also poisoned animals. To control plant
35 diseases he introduced biocides and evidence suggests that bird life was
affected recently by attempts to control dutch elm disease by chemical
means. Biocides killed the insects on which some birds lived and those
who survived the toxicity of the poisons themselves died in large
numbers owing to the reduction in the numbers of insects available.
40   For his own gratification man sought the eggs of the albatross, a bird
which laid only one egg a year. He was greedy for the skins of creatures
like the sea-otter and the seals in spite of the fact that many species
produce only one young every two years. Man's thoughtlessness and
his insatiable greed placed the snowy egret and the ostrich in serious
45 jeopardy because he hunted them for their beautiful plumage and the
cheetah was in danger because humans found its skin very attractive.
   To provide living accommodation and protect himself from malaria
he drained the marshes and in doing so almost eliminated the whoop-
ing-crane which lived there. The mosquito was able to survive man's
50 animosity but certain species of amphibian, such as frogs, toads, and
salamanders, faced eradication. To develop his industry he risked
polluting the atmosphere he and the animals shared. The gases from
the chimneys and the fumes from the factories spoiled and destroyed
the natural habitat of many forms of wild life. To destroy his own kind
55 he exploded nuclear bombs, careless of the effect of radioactive fall-
out on the fauna of his test areas.
   Even when man was not hunting, killing for pleasure, seeking pelts,
and devising new remedies and forms of destruction, man remained
blind to the effects of his behaviour. Rabbits, for example, were
60 deliberately introduced into Australia to provide food but they
multiplied too quickly. Foxes were brought in to control the rabbits
but they turned on the slower, defenceless marsupials rather than
chase the nimble rabbits. Already nine forms of marsupials have been
exterminated and fourteen are under threat today.

EXERCISE FORTY

The following passage is taken from a book on the history of shopping.

a Imagine that you are a historian in the 1980s writing a school text book for use in the fifth forms of secondary schools. *Using only the information given in the passage, give an account in a single paragraph of*:

the reasons for the rise of department stores.

Select the material you need and arrange it to present a convincing statement. *Write in an appropriate style and use clear, correct English.* Use your own words as far as possible; some words cannot be accurately or economically replaced but *do not* copy out long expressions or whole sentences.

Your complete work should not exceed 130 words altogether; *at the end you must state the exact number of words you have used.*

b Write an account for your grown-up children, as if you were the retiring founder of a department store, of:

the ways you and your rivals tried to attract customers to your stores and hold their loyalty.

Use only the information given in the passage and present your account in a single paragraph. Select the material you need and arrange it clearly; *write in correct English and use an appropriate style.* Use your own words as far as possible; some words cannot be accurately or economically replaced but do not copy out long expressions or whole sentences.

Your complete work should not exceed 130 words altogether; *at the end you must state the exact number of words you have used.*

c Imagine that you are a customer living in Victorian times attracted to the new department stores that are appearing. Write a letter to a national newspaper defending them against the charge that they do not give the customer what he or she really wants.

Use only the information given in the passage and present your views clearly; write in correct English and use an appropriate letter form. Use your own words as far as possible; some words cannot be accurately or economically replaced but do not copy out long expressions or whole sentences.

There were obviously certain underlying conditions that enabled department stores to grow up when they did. Before these conditions were ripe, any number of Whiteleys or Harrods must have lived and died small struggling shopkeepers. And now these same conditions
5 impose a certain similarity on them all, in spite of their carefully preserved personalities. From the start they all catered for middle-class customers and set out to convey to them an air of luxury, or at least of solid comfort; 'the subdued and disciplined atmosphere of a gentleman's mansion', as Gordon Selfridge described it when he first
10 came from America. Of necessity, they all arose in central positions where large numbers could reach them easily by the new means of public transport then coming into use. Physically, they grew up in an era of big technical developments in building so that not only could they afford multi-storey palaces (that would have cost a fortune only a
15 few decades before), but they could have enormous plate-glass windows for display, and gas-lighting and novelties like lifts and cash tubes. But, above all, the department stores rose with the rise of the Victorian white-collar workers, the small business and salaried and professional men whose womenfolk had money to spare for a few
20 luxuries and were gradually switching the emphasis of their housekeeping expenditure from food to other kinds of things.
Most stores drew enough customers to fill their huge shops by offering two new things. One was the new manufactures, particularly dress goods and accessories, and household furnishings and equip-
25 ment of all kinds that were coming out of the factories in increasing quantity. The specialist shops stocked these too, of course, but the department stores always made a point of being the first in the field if they could with any novelty in any line. And the other special thing they offered the middle-class shoppers, many of whom were but newly
30 affluent and a little inexperienced in luxury shopping, was a lavish display and a wide choice of these goods.
The department stores, however, introduced into a respectable class of trade the vulgar practice of openly marking or ticketing goods with their price – a practice that has not even yet penetrated to shops with
35 pretensions to being really exclusive. But the department stores as a rule made a virtue not only of displaying their wares as openly as possible but of boldly pricing them for all to see. Their large-scale purchases enabled them to sell cheaply and they were not ashamed in their early days to make price one of their selling points. 'Store prices'
40 were a by-word for cheapness.

100

The lines they concentrated on were fashion goods, things that shoppers were prepared to come some distance for and to take some time and trouble in choosing. The department stores were at least partly responsible for the way the middle-classes gradually became
45 fashion-conscious. They helped to create the demands for which they catered with their ever-changing windows and shop-displays emphasizing 'novelty' and 'up-to-dateness' and 'the latest from the manufacturers'. In a sense they were pulling themselves up by their own boot-straps, for the palatial surroundings, the high degree of
50 service, the sheer quantity and variety of merchandise were all somewhat better than the prices seemed to warrant or than the customers were altogether used to. They were awed and flattered and before they knew it they were influenced and persuaded. Long before the cinema or broadcasting existed, the department stores were
55 helping to mould the tastes of the rising middle-class. And they began also to guide people's steps towards the important new concept of obsolescence; they were the first preachers of the modern creed that goods ought to be replaced when they are out-dated rather than when they are outworn.
60   It has always been the role of department stores to try to cultivate a characteristic atmosphere, even a certain glamour; they have been able to afford carpeted floors and rest-rooms, live Father Christmases in winter, roof gardens in summer. They offer the customer more than mere goods and the customer has been willing to pay the price. 'You
65 know why they come here?' remarked Gordon Selfridge watching the crowds trooping into his store. 'It's so much brighter than their own homes. This is not a shop – it's a community centre.'
   Between the wars the era of department store expansion came to an end, and it is now many years since any big newcomer joined their
70 ranks. The advantages of sheer size on a single site seemed to have reached a limit. Stores strove even harder to attract more customers on to the premises where they would be tempted to buy. The advertising, the store-decorations, the sales events, became extravagantly costly. But the days of their supremacy were over, for new and powerful rivals
75 were appearing.

EXERCISE FORTY-ONE

The following is a school report on the work and attitude of a fifth-former in a comprehensive school. The pupil's first name is given as *K*, so that you may choose whether you take the report to refer to a boy or to a girl.

a   *Using only the information given in the report,* write a comment as if you were the Head of the Year on this pupil's achievements and deficiencies. Your remarks should be justified from the words of your staff colleagues and should refer to the following:

> attitude to work; personal qualities; special features giving pleasure or concern.

Select your material carefully and arrange it in such a way that the pupil is not likely to be discouraged. *Write in full sentences* rather than in notes *and use good, clear, accurate English. Use your own words as far as possible,* but some words and expressions cannot be accurately or economically replaced.

Your comments should not exceed 100 words altogether; *at the end you must state the exact number of words you have used.*

b   Imagine that you are the parent of the pupil to whom the report refers and that you are naturally concerned at some aspects of your child's work and attitude at school. Write a letter to the Headteacher requesting an appointment to discuss the situation and point out the areas of concern raised by the teachers' comments. Do not merely refer to specific subjects in your letter but group and arrange your material to make it clear, as precisely as you can, what general problems are worrying you.

Use only the information and comments contained in the report; do not add ideas of your own. *Write in good, clear, accurate English* and use an appropriate style and form of letter. *Use your own words as far as possible,* but some words and expressions cannot be accurately or economically replaced.

The main body of your letter (i.e. not counting the addresses, the initial 'Dear . . . . .', and the concluding phrases and signature) should not exceed 200 words altogether; *at the end you must state the exact number of words you have used* in the whole letter and how many you have used in the 'main body'.

WOODLEIGH COUNTY SCHOOL

Name: K.N. Scroggins   *Term*: Christmas, 1980
Class: 5H   *Class Teacher*: H.A. Taylor, B.A.

Subject	Grade	Comment	Initials
ART	C	Co-operative in class, but not much real ability; tries hard but no sense of colour or perspective; probably lacks patience to prepare work properly.	KJF
BIOLOGY	C–	Frankly, bored. Not involved in classwork and homework sadly neglected. Neither the theoretical nor the practical aspects of the work evoke much response.	PRN
CHEMISTRY	B	Usually sound but sometimes finds the accurate recording of experiments tedious; observations are hurried and as a result superficial. With greater attention to detail, better results still could be achieved.	LS
ENGLISH LANGUAGE	B	Interested and imaginative; creative writing is promising but the work is spoilt by inaccurate grammar and poor spelling; some problem in seeing relevance and in reading closely. Seems to read widely.	TMH
ENGLISH LITERATURE	B–	An insight into poetry but is not organised sufficiently to cope with the novel. Rather reluctant to take part in dramatic readings in class. Seems rather withdrawn and prefers to read quietly and independently; some evidence of good, critical judgement developing. An interesting but puzzling student.	TMH

103

Subject	Grade	Comment	Initials
~~FRENCH~~/ GEOGRAPHY	C	Enjoys reading about social conditions in other countries but finds the practical work rather tedious. Map-reading is careless and map-making is too sketchy. Rather reluctant to join in class discussion. I wonder why Geography was chosen in preference to French.	ML-J
HISTORY	C–	A disappointing term's work. Clearly has the ability but is unable (or unwilling) to organise and take trouble with notes; facts are jumbled and conclusions confused. Seems to prefer writing fiction.	JFN
MATHE-MATICS	B+	Good; especially able in Algebra and Geometry and quick to see the way through problems. Can think abstractly but finds routine arithmetical calculations tedious. Would find a pocket calculator useful but would almost certainly rely on it too much. Ready to assist slower members of the form when asked.	RA
PHYSICS	B+	An ability here to understand fundamental relationships between causes and effects; enjoys working out what ought to happen and then applying what does happen to the basic problem. Prefers to work individually but will take the lead when working in pairs.	AJ
PHYSICAL EDUCATION	D	A rare mixture of deliberate awkwardness and casual ability. Participates reluctantly in group activities but shows some ability in tennis and swimming. Clumsiness in gymnastics has to be seen to be believed.	AMFB

Subject	Grade	Comment	Initials
RELIGIOUS STUDIES	A	Quickly understands the implications of a moral problem and is prepared to argue convincingly but doggedly from personal experience and conviction. Although the study of Biblical texts sometimes lacks thoroughness, there is ample evidence of an interest in world religions.	RP

Tutor's comment:

K– is obviously having problems of establishing an identity and has not yet settled down to work in a way that augurs well for next summer's GCE examinations. A loyal and reliable member of the group, K– is a strange blend of confidence and shyness.

H.A. Taylor

Head of Year's comment:

EXERCISE FORTY-TWO

The following passage gives an account of one of the most astonishing events in the history of archaeology: the entrance through the sealed door to the tomb of Tutankhamen by Howard Carter on Friday, 17 February, 1922. It is written by Carter, the leader of the excavations. Mace, Callender, Lord Carnarvon, and M. Lacau shared in the event.

a Write an imaginary conversation that might have taken place on the Friday evening, after these four of Carter's friends had returned to their hotel for the night. In the conversation they summarise the main events of the afternoon as they saw them *from their own points of view.*

Use only the information given in the passage; do not add ideas of your own. Select the material and re-arrange it effectively so that differences in viewpoints become clear. Use an appropriate style for a conversation but *write in good, clear, accurate English. Do not try to summarise everything in the passage,* but choose only the main events. You should set out the work in the form of a dialogue; select an appropriate form and then be consistent in the way you set it out.

The complete conversation should not exceed 250 words in length; *at the end you must state accurately the number of words you have used.*

b Write a factual account of the events of the afternoon on Friday, 17 February, 1922, for publication as the main article in *The Times* on Saturday, 18 February, 1922. The article should try to convey the facts and the importance of the discovery. If you can, introduce into the account something of the excitement felt by those who were present.

For your account use only the information given in the passage; do not add ideas of your own. Select the material you need and arrange it economically. *Write in an appropriate style* and use good, clear, accurate English.

Your complete article should not exceed 200 words in length; *at the end you must state accurately the exact number of words you have used.*

By the middle of February our work in the Antechamber was finished. With the exception of the two sentinel statues, left for a special reason, all its contents had been removed to the laboratory, every inch of its floor had been swept and sifted for the last bead or fallen piece of inlay, 5 and it now stood bare and empty. We were ready at last to penetrate the mystery of the sealed door.

Friday, the 17th, was the day appointed, and at two o'clock those who were to be privileged to witness the ceremony met by appointment above the tomb. They included Lord Carnarvon, Lady Evelyn 10 Herbert, H.E. Abd el Halim Pasha Suleman, Minister of Public Works, M. Lacau, Director-General of the Service of Antiquities, Sir William Garstin, Sir Charles Cust, Mr Lythgoe, Curator of the Egyptian Department of the Metropolitan Museum, New York, Professor Breasted, Dr Alan Gardiner, Mr Winlock, the Hon. Mervyn 15 Herbert, the Hon. Richard Bethell, Mr Engelbach, Chief Inspector of the Department of Antiquities, three Egyptian inspectors of the Department of Antiquities, the representative of the Government Press Bureau, and the members of the staff – about twenty persons in all. By a quarter past two the whole company had assembled, so we 20 removed our coats and filed down the sloping passage into the tomb.

In the Antechamber everything was prepared and ready, and to those who had not visited it since the original opening of the tomb it must have presented a strange sight. We had screened the statues with 25 boarding to protect them from possible damage, and between them we had erected a small platform, just high enough to enable us to reach the upper part of the doorway, having determined, as the safest plan, to work from the top downwards. A short distance back from the platform there was a barrier, and beyond, knowing that there might be 30 hours of work ahead of us, we had provided chairs for the visitors. On either side standards had been set up for our lamps, their light shining full upon the doorway. Looking back, we realize what a strange, incongruous picture the chamber must have presented, but at the time I question whether such an idea even crossed our minds. One thought 35 and one only was possible. There before us lay the sealed door, and with its opening we were to blot out the centuries and stand in the presence of a king who reigned three thousand years ago. My own feelings as I mounted the platform were a strange mixture, and it was with a trembling hand that I struck the first blow.

40 My first care was to locate the wooden lintel above the door: then very carefully I chipped away the plaster and picked out the small stones which formed the uppermost layer of the filling. The temptation to stop and peer inside at every moment was irresistible, and when, after about ten minutes' work, I had made a hole large enough to 45 enable me to do so, I inserted an electric torch. An astonishing sight its light revealed, for there, within a yard of the doorway, stretching as far

as one could see and blocking the entrance to the chamber, stood what
to all appearance was a solid wall of gold. For the moment there was
no clue as to its meaning, so as quickly as I dared I set to work to widen
50 the hole. This had now become an operation of considerable difficulty,
for the stones of the masonry were not accurately squared blocks built
regularly upon one another, but rough slabs of varying size, some so
heavy that it took all one's strength to lift them: many of them, too, as
the weight above was removed, were left so precariously balanced that
55 the least false movement would have sent them sliding inwards to crash
upon the contents of the chamber below. We were also endeavouring
to preserve the seal-impressions upon the thick mortar of the outer
face, and this added considerably to the difficulty of handling the
stones. Mace and Callender were helping me by this time, and each
60 stone was cleared on a regular system. With a crowbar I gently eased it
up, Mace holding it to prevent it falling forwards; then he and I lifted it
out and passed it back to Callender, who transferred it on to one of the
foremen, and so, by a chain of workmen, up the passage and out of the
tomb altogether.
65   With the removal of a very few stones the mystery of the golden wall
was solved. We were at the entrance of the actual burial-chamber of the
king, and that which barred our way was the side of an immense gilt
shrine built to cover and protect the sarcophagus. It was visible now
from the Antechamber by the light of the standard lamps, and as stone
70 after stone was removed, and its gilded surface came gradually into
view, we could, as though by electric current, feel the tingle of
excitement which thrilled the spectators behind the barrier. We who
were doing the work were probably less excited, for our whole energies
were taken up with the task in hand – that of removing the blocking
75 without an accident. The fall of a single stone might have done
irreparable damage to the delicate surface of the shrine, so, directly the
hole was large enough, we made an additional protection for it by
inserting a mattress on the inner side of the door-blocking, suspending
it from the wooden lintel of the doorway. Two hours of hard work it
80 took us to clear away the blocking, or at least as much of it as was
necessary for the moment; and at one point, when near the bottom, we
had to delay operations for a space while we collected the scattered
beads from a necklace brought by the plunderers from the chamber
within and dropped upon the threshold. This last was a terrible trial to
85 our patience, for it was a slow business, and we were all of us excited to
see what might be within; but finally it was done, the last stones
were removed, and the way to the innermost chamber lay open before
us.
   In clearing away the blocking of the doorway we had discovered that
90 the level of the inner chamber was about four feet lower than that of the

Antechamber, and this, combined with the fact that there was but a narrow space between door and shrine, made an entrance by no means easy to effect. Fortunately, there were no smaller antiquities at this end of the chamber, so I lowered myself down, and then, taking one of the portable lights, I edged cautiously to the corner of the shrine and looked beyond it. At the corner two beautiful alabaster vases blocked the way, but I could see that if these were removed we should have a clear path to the other end of the chamber; so, carefully marking the spot on which they stood, I picked them up – with the exception of the king's wishing-cup they were of finer quality and more graceful shape than any we had yet found – and passed them back to the Antechamber. Lord Carnarvon and M. Lacau now joined me, and, picking our way along the narrow passage between shrine and wall, paying out the wire of our light behind us, we investigated further.

It was, beyond any question, the sepulchral chamber in which we stood, for there, towering above us, was one of the great gilt shrines beneath which kings were laid. So enormous was this structure (17 feet by 11 feet, and 9 feet high, we found afterwards) that it filled within a little the entire area of the chamber, a space of some two feet only separating it from the walls on all four sides, while its roof, with cornice top and torus moulding, reached almost to the ceiling. From top to bottom it was overlaid with gold, and upon its sides there were inlaid panels of brilliant blue faience, in which were represented, repeated over and over, the magic symbols which would ensure its strength and safety. Around the shrine, resting upon the ground, there were a number of funerary emblems, and, at the north end, the seven magic oars the king would need to ferry himself across the waters of the underworld. The walls of the chamber, unlike those of the Antechamber, were decorated with brightly painted scenes and inscriptions, brilliant in their colours, but evidently somewhat hastily executed.

These last details we must have noticed subsequently, for at the time our one thought was of the shrine and of its safety. Had the thieves penetrated within it and disturbed the royal burial? Here, on the eastern end, were the great folding doors, closed and bolted, but not sealed, that would answer the question for us. Eagerly we drew the bolts, swung back the doors, and there within was a second shrine with similar bolted doors, and upon the bolts a seal, intact. This seal we determined not to break, for our doubts were resolved, and we could not penetrate further without risk of serious damage to the monument. I think at the moment we did not even want to break the seal, for a feeling of intrusion had descended heavily upon us with the opening of the doors. We felt that we were in the presence of the dead king and must do him reverence.

EXERCISE FORTY-THREE

The following extracts are taken from the diary of a Lancashire weaver, John O'Neil. The diary was written in a cash book found on a rubbish heap. Its entries cover the years 1860–1864 and deal with the effects on the town of Clitheroe of the cotton famine caused by the American Civil War. O'Neil was a lifelong Liberal, a strong supporter of reading-rooms for workers, mechanics' institutes, and trades unions.

a *Using only the information contained in the diary's entries,* write a summary for an article to be published in the local history column of a Lancashire local newspaper of:

> the causes and effects of the cotton famine on John O'Neil and his fellow workers in Clitheroe during 1864.

Select and arrange the relevant material for your article in not more than three paragraphs. *Write in good, clear, and accurate English* and use an appropriate style. *Use your own words as far as possible,* although some words and expressions cannot be accurately or economically replaced. Your complete article should not exceed 200 words altogether; *at the end you must state the exact number of words you have used.*

b *Using only the information contained in the diary's entries,* write a personal statement *in two paragraphs* that might have been produced by John O'Neil and addressed to his employers in order to persuade them to improve the wages and work conditions. Your paragraphs should set out:

i the hardships he has had to suffer whilst at work; *and*

ii the difficulties he and his fellow workers endure in their personal daily lives.

Write in good, clear, and accurate English and use an appropriate style. Use your own words as far as possible, although some words and expressions cannot be accurately or economically replaced. Your complete statement should not exceed 175 words altogether; *at the end you must state the exact number of words you have used.*

c *Using only the information contained in the diary's entries,* write an account *in two paragraphs* suitable for inclusion in a history text book of:

i the political and military events that took place in America in 1864; *and*

ii the events of historical importance that took place on the Continent of Europe in 1864.

Write in good, clear, and accurate English and use an appropriate style. Use your own words as far as possible, although some words and expressions cannot be accurately or economically replaced. Your complete account should not exceed 150 words altogether; *at the end you must state the exact number of words you have used.*

April 1864

10th It is nearly two years since I wrote anything in the way of a diary. I now take up my pen to resume the task. It has been a very poor time for me all the time owing to the American war, which seems as far off being settled as ever. The mill I work in was stopped all last
5 winter, during which time I had 3s. per week allowed by the relief committee, which barely kept me alive. When we started work again it was with Surat cotton, and a great number of weavers can only mind two looms. We can earn very little. I have not earned a shilling a day this last month, and there are many like me. My clothes and
10 bedding are wearing out very fast and I have no means of getting any more, as what wages I get hardly keep me, my daughter and son-in-law having gone to a house of their own during the time I was out of work. I went twice to Preston to see my brother Daniel, but he and his family were no better off than myself, having nothing better than
15 Surat[1] to work at, and it is the same all through Lancashire. There has been some terrible and bloody battles fought in America these last two years. . . The principal reason why I did not take any notes these last two years is because I was sad and weary. One half of the time I was out of work and the other I had to work as hard as ever I wrought
20 in my life, and can hardly keep myself living. If things do not mend this summer I will try somewhere else or something else, for I can't go much further with what I am at.

17th I have had another weary week of bad work. I have just earned
25 7s. 3½d. off three looms and there are plenty as bad off as me, and if any one complains to the Master of bad work he says, if you don't like

---

[1] *Surat*: a coarse, uncoloured cotton, so-called from *Surat*, in India

[it] you can leave. He wants no one to stop that does not like it, and that is all the satisfaction we can get...

May

30 **1st** There has been some little rain today, the first we have had for three weeks. It is much wanted ... I have given up my odd loom as I cannot keep two looms going, and last week I had only 5s 1½d. after a very hard week's work, but they have promised us better work as soon as the cotton is done that they have on hand. They have
35 promised so often that we can hardly believe them.

8th We have had a very fine week of sunshine and showers, and everything is growing very fast in fields and gardens, and markets are coming down very fast... The work at our place is beginning to mend. I have got two beams[1] in, the best I have had for twelve
40 months, but they are for shifting the looms out of our shop into a new shed that is ready for starting, so I hope to get better on than I have done this last winter. In Denmark the Danes are retreating and the Austrians and Prussians are advancing. There is a conference sitting in London on the war, but how it will end there is no one knows.

45 **15th** Whitsunday. It has been very hot all day and I have been out walking nearly all afternoon. The news from America gives an account of the defeat of the Federal army under General Banks on the Red River with the loss of 4000 men and twenty pieces of cannon, and in the course of another week we may hear of one of the greatest
50 battles that ever was fought... At home things are much about the same. I have been shifted into the new shed and got two very bad looms and bad work in them, so I am no better off than I was. We are to have a holiday tomorrow, but I am too poor to go anywhere so I must stay at home.

55 **22nd** It has been very hot all this week, with some thunder showers. I have been walking all this afternoon, and everything looks well in fields and gardens, with every prospect of a good fruit year... In Denmark all is quiet just now, and the Polish insurrection is over and many hundreds of families are sent to Siberia; and at our mill things are
60 likely to get worse. The spinners turned out, and a deputation waited upon the Masters, wanting them to mend the work as it was so bad they could scarce get a living. The Masters said they would not mend it and if they did not like it they could leave, so they had to go work again.

[1] *beams*: cylinders of wood in a loom

65 **29th** Another week of bad work. It is as bad now as ever it was, and no signs of it mending. . .

June

19th It has been fine growing weather this last week, and hay harvest has commenced. . . In Europe the Danish armistice [is] prolonged
70 another fortnight, and if nothing definite is come to, there will be war again; and at Low Moor things are as bad as ever. I went up to Clitheroe last night. There was a great temperance demonstration and procession which passed off very well. New potatoes were selling at two pound for 3½d.

75 **26th** There has been a great deal of rain this last week and today is very cold and boisterous. . . There was a great battle fought last Sunday morning off the French coast near Cherbourg between the Federal war steamer *Kearsa[r]ge* and the Confederate cruiser the *Alabama,* which had burned and destroyed one hundred
80 merchantmen belonging to the United States. The fight lasted an hour and ten minutes when the rebel ship was sent to the bottom. The captain and some of the officers escaped on board an English yacht that came out of Cherbourg with her. They had eleven killed and twenty wounded, and about ten or a dozen were drowned, along with
85 the surgeon; while the *Kearsage* was very little damaged and had only three men wounded. They picked up sixty-eight men from the sinking ship. . . In Clitheroe last night new potatoes were selling five pounds for 6d., so I got some for my dinner and came home again.

July

90 **10th** It has been very fine warm weather since Wednesday, and a great deal of hay has been got in in good condition. . . In Denmark the Prussians are taking every place they come to, the Danes offering very little resistance. In Parliament the Tories brought forward a motion for a vote of censure upon the Government for the way they
95 have treated the Danish question. The debate lasted all week, and on a division the Ministers had a majority of eighteen. There is no other news of importance this week. . .

August

14th This has been a fine warm week and we stopped yesterday as the
00 engine wanted repairs, so I whitewashed and cleaned the house and today I am very stiff and tired. The latest news from America shews that Sherman has not captured Atlanta but that he has invested[1] it

---

[1] *invested*: laid siege to

with a view to make it surrender; and General Grant has blown up a
fort at Petersburg with a rebel regiment and had taken the outer line
105 of defences. There is nothing else of importance... At our mill we
have had two turn-outs for bad work. It has been getting worse all
summer until we could stand it no longer, and the last time we were
out we stopped out all day, when the Master told the deputation that
waited upon him that he would work his present stock of cotton up
110 and then he would buy better sorts and have as good work as any in
Clitheroe. It is shameful the work we have in at present. I had only 6s.
this last week with very hard work, and there was some had less than
me; and then our machinery is running very slow owing to the great
drought as Ribble is very near dry. We have had frosty nights and
115 warm days this last fortnight, and harvest has been commenced. There
were thirty mills stopped in Blackburn this last week for want of
water, and will not start again until wet weather sets in. I don't know
that there is anything else of importance.

September

120 **11th** We have had a week of very wet weather which was much
wanted... Things are much about the same at Atlanta and Mobile,
but the principal news from America just now is the coming election
for President, because it depends upon which of the candidates is
chosen whether there will be peace or a continuance of the war, and as
125 the position of the parties are about evenly balanced there is no
knowing yet how things may be, because if there should be peace,
then the price of cotton must come down 2s. per pound, and that is
the reason why the cotton trade is so bad just now. The merchants
will not buy cloth, as they expect the price will come down one half,
130 and the Manufacturers will not buy cotton for the same reason. There
are several mills in Lancashire begun to run short time and some are
stopping altogether. At our mills the cotton was done last Tuesday
and no signs of any coming. There is none working now but weavers,
and if no cotton comes, why then, we must stop next, so everything
135 has a black look – and winter coming on!

18th Another wet week and bad prospects for trade. We got as much
cotton last week as kept the mill running two days and a half, and as
cotton has come down 4d. per pound it is thought we may get some
more... The Chicago convention have met and have put General
140 M'Clellan in nomination as President in opposition to Abraham
Lincoln, so now both sides are fairly at work, and as the election
comes off on the fourth of November the cotton trade in the
meanwhile will be greatly depressed until the result is known.

25th We have had some fine weather these days, and harvest is nearly
145 over... The cotton trade is getting worse every day. There is no
market whatever, and mills are closing every day. The weft[1] we have
had this last week is worse than ever, but we are forced to put up with
it, as we don't know how soon we will have to stop altogether.

October

150 **2nd** It has been very fine all week and things are looking very bad. At
our mill they are all working three days a week, except the weavers,
who are yet on full time; but as the material is very bad they make
very little wages. I have given up my odd loom and I find that two is as
many as I can manage with such bad weft. There is a complete
155 stagnation in trade, both in the cotton and cloth market, and nothing
doing...

9th Another fine week and very little doing. There has been nothing
but the weavers working at our mill this week. All the rest are doing
nothing, but they have got some cotton which will last three days, and
160 all have to start tomorrow morning... There is great distress all
through Lancashire at present owing to so many mills stopping, and
Clitheroe will soon be as bad as anywhere else.

16th We commenced short time last Monday, and on Thursday we
stopped altogether and does not know when we will start again. The
165 cotton that was bought last week – about forty bales – fell a penny a
pound about two hours after he had bought it and he will buy no
more until the market settles. I should have gone to Preston this
morning but it was so wet, but I shall go tomorrow if all be well...

23rd We have been stopped all week and likely for stopping a little
170 longer as there is no cotton bought yet, although it has fallen 2 pence
per pound last week, but in the cloth market there is nothing doing
whatever. I went to Preston last Monday but only to find that my
brother and family had left last Whitsuntide owing to the mill they
were working in stopping. They have gone to Dolphinholme near
175 Lancaster and never sent me word. I saw McMurray and family, who
gave me all the information, so I found it was no use stopping there so
I walked all the way to Blackburn [ten miles] and took the train to
Clitheroe. It has been very stormy all week and we have had little
pleasure. I applied with several others to the Relief Committee
180 yesterday and got 3s., and our Masters gave every hand 2s., so we are
not so badly off this week, whatever they may do next week. It was

[1] *weft*: the threads woven into and crossing the warp (the threads stretched out
lengthwise on a loom).

115

the great fair yesterday, and a very poor one it was owing to the stormy weather and so many people out of work. The news from America is much about the same as last week, very little doing on either side. The friends of Mr Lincoln say they are sure of winning the election by a large majority[1].

30th We commenced work last Thursday and started full time, as our Masters have bought a large supply of cotton which will last a few weeks; and the cloth market is a trifle better this last week and it is thought that it has got a turn for the better. . . The public mind is taken up with the Presidential contest, both sides say they are sure of winning, but in a week or two we shall know all about it. There is nothing else of any importance.

November

6th The weavers have been on full time all week, but the rest of the hands have only had four days and the markets are as gloomy as ever. . .

December

4th There is very little news of any kind lately that I have made no note of it. Lincoln has been re-elected President of America and there has been nothing but skirmishing since, and it is likely that there will not be much done until spring. At home we have nothing but stormy weather and bad work, and a poor prospect for Christmas.

[1] They did – 2,216,076 for Lincoln and 1,808,725 for M'Clellan.

EXERCISE FORTY-FOUR

The following passage is taken from an article, first published in 1863, describing the work done by young women at coal mines.

a Write a summary, as if written by a history teacher for a class of sixteen-year-olds, setting out clearly and concisely:

  the details of the work done by the young women.

  Your summary should be as factual as possible, and should use only the information provided in the passage. *Write in correct English and use your own words as far as possible*; some words and expressions cannot be accurately or economically replaced but do not copy out long expressions or whole sentences.

  Your summary should be *a single paragraph not more than 60 words in length. At the end you must state the number of words you have used.*

b Imagine that you are a mine-owner of the time and have been criticised for the way you employ young women. Write an article for a serious magazine justifying your use of young women for such work.

  Use only the information provided in the passage; do not add ideas of your own. Write in correct English and use an appropriate style. Use your own words as far as possible; some words and expressions cannot be accurately or economically replaced but do not copy out long expressions or whole sentences.

  You should not use more than two paragraphs or exceed 120 words altogether; at the end you must state the number of words you have used.

c Write a letter to a national newspaper of 1863 deploring the way in which the young women are employed. Give reasons to support your view and offer suggestions how the women's way of life could be improved.

  Use only the information provided in the passage; do not add ideas of your own. Write in correct English and use an appropriate form of letter. Use your own words as far as possible; some words and expressions cannot be accurately or economically replaced but do not copy out long expressions or whole sentences.

The body of your letter, which may be written in two paragraphs, *should not exceed 120 words in length; at the end you must state the number of words you have used.*

Of the groups engaged above-ground, the most remarkable are composed of the young women who are at work on the pit-mounds: they take charge of the 'skips', or baskets of coal and ironstone, when they are landed on the bank. They load the coal in trucks to be carried
5 off to its destination. They separate the ironstone from the shale, which is wheeled off to the extremity of the gradually increasing mound, and they send off the ore to be stacked in large quadrangular heaps, where it is left to undergo, for a while, the cleansing influence of the atmosphere. This is heavy and dirty work, and the pit-girls who
10 are engaged in it, with their shabby dresses tied grotesquely about them, and their inverted bonnets stuck on the top of their heads, seem not less sordid. But before the onlooker draws his conclusions, let him see them on a Sunday with clean persons, bright complexions, sparkling eyes, and dressed out in the cheap finery which now-a-days
15 levels all distinctions of costume.

The labour of the pit-mound is severe, and is not regularly undertaken by those who are mothers; but the workwomen have an air of robust health, and the beauty and number of the children in the cottages prove that the constitution of the mothers has not been
20 injured by over-work in early life. 'Huge women' are they, flushed with sun, and wind, and rain, and labour. But strange to say, there are to be found among them forms of great refinement and delicacy.

Pit-mound labour is stigmatised by many well-meaning reformers as not only 'unfeminine', but also conducive to immorality. But to
25 this we demur. No occupation, indeed, which involves hard work can be considered feminine. Domestic drudgery is feminine only because in England we are accustomed to impose it on women. God forbid that we should advocate the employment of women in any hard work which can be spared them! The revelations of the Commission
30 appointed to inquire into the condition of women employed in the mines may well excite our jealousy on all such subjects, and too much praise cannot be given to the exertions which the Duke of Buccleugh and other proprietors have made to prevent the employment of women in the pits. But the labour on the pit-mound in the open air is
35 not degrading, it does not bring the workwomen into unseemly association with the men, nor does it expose them to the contamina-

tion of coarse language. They hear on the pit-mounds exactly the language they would hear at home, and much less of it, for work is not favourable to conversation. Regular occupation, and habits of
40 independence and self-protection, are not unfavourable to the preservation of female virtue among the working classes; and in fact statistical returns prove that the morality of the colliery is quite equal to that of any rural district. Much may be done to improve the condition of the poor pit-girl, but it would be an ill beginning to
45 deprive her of her bread.

Nothing would be more desirable than to give the future mistress of the collier's cottage some instruction in the arts of housewifery. A little knowledge of cookery not only adds very greatly to the comfort of the collier's home, but may become a source of considerable profit.
50 We once knew a poor widow, who thought herself without resource, but subsequently maintained herself in what she considered opulence, by making tea-cakes which fortunately hit the public taste. The only experiment of the kind, which we have seen tried, was to employ the school girls in turn to work in a soup-kitchen which had
55 been established, not as a charity, but as a means of supplying the people with wholesome food: and hitherto it has met with imperfect success. In one instance, evening meetings of the pit-girls have been set on foot by kind ladies who attend to teach them to sew and cut out, and also to read to them, and instruct them, while they are at
60 their work. The professed object of the meeting is to make clothes of various kinds which may be purchased by the pit-girls themselves, or others of the work-people, at cost price. This attempt has met with a more complete and more rapid success than usually attends measures of colliery reform.

EXERCISE FORTY-FIVE

The following passage is taken from a book about the British seaside.

a A friend of your family has just returned to Britain after twenty years abroad, and has written to you inviting you to go on a seaside holiday.

Write a letter in reply in which you point out what is likely to be the same about any seaside resort and what changes are likely to be found after the twenty-year absence.

Use only the information to be found in the passage; do not introduce ideas of your own. Write in correct English and use your own words as far as possible. Some words and expressions cannot be accurately or economically replaced but do not copy out long expressions or whole sentences.

Use an appropriate form for your letter. *The body of your letter should not be more than 110 words long. At the end state the number of words you have used.*

b You are an Entertainments Officer at a seaside resort keen to attract holidaymakers to your resort. Write a report for the Council who employ you, setting out:

i what can be predicted about holidaymakers' behaviour and likes and dislikes; *and*

ii what your resort ought to provide to be attractive to visitors.

Your report should use only the information given in the passage. Write in correct English and use your own words as far as possible; some words and expressions cannot be accurately or economically replaced but do not copy out long expressions or whole sentences.

Your report should be set out in *two paragraphs,* one for each topic. The paragraphs need not be evenly balanced, but *your report should not exceed 140 words in total. State at the end the number of words you have used.*

Sunbathing, swimming, and lounging on a beach are now essential attributes of a seaside holiday, but the statistics on climate do not seem to have undermined the attraction of the colder northern

resorts. Weather statistics prove conclusively that the south coast
5 enjoys more sunshine than other coastal areas. Brighton, for example, has 256 hours more sunshine each year than Blackpool. But
whereas Brighton attracts 4-5 million visitors, Blackpool continues
to boast of 7 million. Moreover, the English continue to flock to the
coast in their greatest numbers in August, although that is not the
10 best English summer month for low rainfall and plenty of sunshine. It
is true, of course, that for many people, particularly those with a car,
the weather is now an important factor. If the day's weather forecast
predicts gloom along the coast, it is scarcely worth setting out for a
day's trip. On the other hand, even the brightest of weather forecasts
15 will scarcely persuade people to drive 300 miles from Yorkshire to the
south coast rather than, say, to Scarborough. People tend to plan
their holidays well in advance, knowing that in their limited free time
there will be severe competition from tens of thousands of people for
space and accommodation. When arranging an English holiday
20 months ahead, there is no guarantee that the weather will be fine.
Even those who decide to use their homes as a base for a series of day-
trips often make that decision well in advance, though for them it
seems that the daily weather forecasts are important. Many people
resolve their doubts about the English summer by flying to the
25 Mediterranean.

English seaside resorts have, since the inter-war years, spent large
amounts of money in promoting their sunny image, but it is unclear
how such publicity has altered the contours of English holiday-
making. Although more people have turned to Spain and other
30 European resorts, the statistics of visitors to the English coastal
towns scarcely suggest a collapse in their popularity. Resorts may
differ greatly from one another, but the nature of social life has
remained remarkably steady, despite the impact of prosperity. The
1960s and 1970s have seen a continuation of the process, first
35 discernible a century before, of commercial changes slowly reshaping
the physical face of the resorts, in order to provide visitors with what
they wanted and were familiar with. Certain features remain apparently unalterable. The English seaside is unthinkable without
donkeys, buckets and spades, ice-cream and sea-food stalls. But the
40 commercial face of the popular resorts has experienced major
changes. In particular, television has transformed seaside entertainment, and it is worth noting that the television companies present a
number of shows and 'spectaculars' direct from the seaside.

The impact of television on seaside entertainment is similar to that
45 made, in the previous century, by the music-hall. Before the First
World War, the major resorts were able to attract highly paid music-
hall stars; today, the new stars of television also find themselves

121

drawn to the resorts in the summer. The seaside visitors want not the
new and unfamiliar, but the known and proven; and the resorts give
50 them what they want. This applies particularly to the bingo halls
which, though commonplace throughout the land, find in the resorts
some of their prime positions and an even more guaranteed prosperity. There has been an amazing development of entertainment
gadgetry at the seaside, not confined to the piers. New materials and
55 cheap forms of manufacture have enabled leisure industries to
'develop' whole sites into new fun-palaces, with structures of foam,
plastic and polythene. Visitors, returning after an absence of twenty
years, are greeted by virtually different towns, although urban
renewal is no worse at the resorts than in other English towns.
60   One of the most important social changes in English cultural
patterns since the early 1960s has been the proliferation of
restaurants and eating-places, frequently pioneered by the Chinese.
The resulting expansion of eating-houses and the national chains of
restaurants have found a suitable market in the resorts. This is not a
65 complete innovation, for cooked food had long been available at the
seaside. Before 1914, working-class visitors were faced with a greater
variety of cheap cooked foods than they could ever have found in
their home towns. However, catering has now entered the world of
big business; and seaside restaurants, like cars, costly shows, expen-
70 sive drinking habits and gambling saloons, have become signs and
symptoms of a society with a large amount of surplus cash readily
available for the pursuit of leisure. Resorts are in essence urban
monuments to the pursuit of mass leisure; more recently, that leisure
has become more varied, spectacular and colourfully seductive.

The following passage is taken from a study of the uses cathedrals are put to.

a   A church-going friend of yours has expressed misgivings about the value of cathedrals as places of worship compared with local parish churches. Write a reply to that friend, which would be printed in your parish magazine, pointing out the part still played by cathedrals in worship.

Use only the information given in the passage. Write in correct English and use your own words as far as possible. Some words and expressions cannot be accurately or economically replaced but do not copy out long expressions or whole sentences.

You should use *one paragraph not more than 90 words in length. State at the end the number of words you have used.*

b   You are employed by a tourist office and have to write an article on the attractions and benefits of visiting cathedrals. The tourist magazine in which it will be published is intended for British holidaymakers and also for visitors from abroad.

Your article should use only the information provided in the passage. Write in clear and correct English and use your own words as far as possible. Do not copy out long expressions or whole sentences which could be better replaced.

Your article should not be more than 150 words in length. At the end you should state the number of words you have used.

c   You have read an article in a national newspaper which says that the upkeep of cathedrals is a waste of money. Write a letter to that newspaper in reply, pointing out the value and uses of cathedrals and justifying their continued existence.

Draw on the information provided in the passage and do not introduce ideas of your own. Write in correct English and use your own words as far as possible.

Use an appropriate layout for your letter. *The body of your letter should not exceed 140 words in length. State at the end the number of words you have used.*

Cathedrals are amongst the oldest and finest buildings in Britain, and it is natural that they should attract large numbers of visitors.

Westminster Abbey, St Paul's, and Canterbury Cathedral all give figures in the region of three million visitors annually, and it is
5 evident on a most superficial glance that these three buildings are sometimes overcrowded. The nave of Canterbury on many days during the summer resembles nothing so much as Wembley on Cup Final day, and many of the visitors are clearly from abroad. York estimates that it has approximately two million visitors annually,
10 though so vast is the Minster that the feeling of being overcrowded is apparently rare. Possibly because they are open every day of the year as part of their primary purpose, namely religious worship, cathedrals attract far more visitors than the most successful stately homes opened specially to the public.
15 Why should this be? The reasons are many and varied. Uppermost must be the sheer quality of the buildings – think of Salisbury, Durham, and York – which is sufficient to remind us of the level of medieval achievement in building them, and in creating the wealth of medieval or later stained glass, woodwork, sculpture and metalwork
20 which adorn them. Moreover, these buildings tend to be situated in natural centres of areas, typical being Exeter, Bristol and Norwich. Here they continue to have a significant role as a focus for the diocese and county, and this must in itself account for many local visits. There are reports of cathedrals being visited again and again by
25 people living in the locality.
It is an admitted phenomenon that visitors to stately homes prefer houses which are lived in to those that are not; so it is with cathedrals – the more visitors they receive the more they seem ready to respond, and to be 'alive', and the more alive they are the more visitors they
30 attract. The splendidly maintained choral services are often very well attended, and act as a tangible reminder that worship lies at the centre of a cathedral's existence. Some cathedrals – Truro, Winchester, Carlisle and Chichester – are so situated that they form ready made 'wet day' activities for tourists who throng through the cathedral city.
35 Such cathedrals report a marked increase in visitors on days when bad weather prevents families visiting the seaside or going on to the surrounding moors. The recognition element can also be important. Most of us have grown up knowing all our lives about York, St Paul's, and Canterbury. To visit them when opportunities occur is
40 therefore a natural, almost inevitable, consequence in a way which is not true of country houses.
Cathedrals are not only centres of artistic excellence but of spiritual power: the man who would feel embarrassed and lost if it ever occurred to him to visit his parish church frequently finds the
45 great scale of the cathedral all-welcoming, and something touches him and moves him about the values which the cathedral has stood

for and represented for so long. The procession of choir and clergy may take some visitors by surprise, but it is remarkable how many take evident pleasure in the beauty of the music and the spoken
50 service, married to superb architecture. Not only is there generally no entry fee to cathedrals, but there is no sense of pressure, no hard-sell and no time limit. You have to leave when the cathedral closes for the night, but otherwise the place is your own. Whether for old or young, a cathedral has a special attraction as a 'momentary monastery' – not
55 quite a withdrawal from the world but an opportunity to relax, step aside from ordinary distractions, if only for a few minutes.

In addition to drawing the casual visitor, cathedrals are also used as the settings for special attractions. Festivals linked with the seasons of the year, such as flower and harvest time, bring colour to
60 the aisles, while sometimes there are musical and dramatic performances. For example, the Three Choirs Festival, which rotates between Gloucester, Hereford and Worcester cathedrals, is the oldest established music festival in the world. Cathedrals also attract organized visits with a special purpose, particularly from schools. St
65 Alban's, for example, has six hundred or so annual school visits, in addition to an annual youth festival. Cathedrals also have an educational role in a broader sense. From the earliest times they have been centres of learning, and many of them still have outstanding libraries. The library at Lincoln was designed by Sir Christopher
70 Wren; that at Winchester has occupied the same room since the twelfth century. The same sense of continuity is felt at Exeter, with its collection of Anglo-Saxon manuscripts, and at Salisbury and Lincoln with their copies of the Magna Carta. With treasures like these cathedrals can scarcely fail to attract visitors.

NOTES (see page 19)

Suggested notes for summarising the passage on the Namib Desert
1 The beautiful Namib Desert in south-west Africa
2 is five hundred miles wide with very high dunes
3 and adjoins a wild ocean.
4 It has high day-time temperatures and no rain.
5 Yet tracks in the sand show that a variety of wild life abounds there
6 and such life needs moisture.
7 Each day the desert has thick fog
8 caused by the cold air above an Antarctic current meeting the hot desert air.
9 The fog leaves droplets of water
10 which the wild life lives off.

Acknowledgements

For permission to use and in some cases slightly edit or adapt copyright material grateful thanks are due to the following:

University of London University Entrance and School Examinations Council for passages used in the following exercises – exercise 1 (adapted from *Human Groups* by W. J. H. Sprott, 1958, Penguin Books Ltd, pp. 78–81), exercise 2 (adapted from 'The New World of Children' by J. H. Plumb *The Listener* of 26 February 1976), exercise 3, exercise 4, exercise 5 and exercise 36; Mr Colin Willock and Survival Anglia Ltd for an extract from an article on the Namib Desert, the *TV Times* of 6 September 1973; The Associated Examining Board for passages used in the following exercises – exercise 7 (adapted from *Children's Games in Street and Playground* by Iona and Peter Opie, 1969, Oxford University Press), exercise 8 (adapted from *The Wreck Hunters* by R. Jefferis and K.McDonald, 1966, George G. Harrap & Co Ltd), exercise 9 (adapted from *Zoos of the World* by James Fisher, 1966, Aldus Books London), exercise 10 (adapted from *The Practice of Journalism* by J. Dodge and G. Viner, 1963, William Heinemann Ltd); FAB 208 for the first three letters in exercise 13; D. C. Thomson & Co Ltd for the fourth letter in exercise 13; Frederick Warne Ltd for the maps in exercise 15 from *A World Atlas of Military History* by Arthur Banks, 1974; the *Sunday Times Magazine* of 27 January 1980 for the table of British Rail accomplishments; Pitman Publishing Ltd for an extract from *Dictionary of the World's Mammals* by M.Burton; Macmillan Publishers Ltd for an extract from *Shoplifting: Controlling a Major Crime* by D. P. Walsh, 1978; Hodder & Stoughton Ltd for an extract from *Encyclopaedia of Dates and Events* by Pascoe, Lee and Jenkins, © 1968, 1974 by Hodder & Stoughton Ltd; *Encyclopaedia Britannica* for an extract from 'Women, Status of' *Encyclopaedia Britannica*, 15th edition (1974); Intasun North Ltd for an extract from their 1980 summer holiday brochure on the Grand Bahama; Thomson Holidays for an extract from their 1980 holiday brochure; Vallentine, Mitchell & Co Ltd, London for an extract from *The Diary of Anne Frank*, 4 r.e. 1971; John Murray (Publishers) Ltd for an extract from *Technological Eating* by M.Pyke, 1972; Her Majesty's Stationery Office for tables from *Schools Council Enquiry 1* by R.Morton Williams and S.Finch, 1968; the *Radio Times* of 22 December 1979 for an extract from 'Sport on Television' by Brian Glanville; William Heinemann Ltd for an extract from *A New Look at Dinosaurs* by Alan Charig, 1979; Routledge & Kegan Paul Ltd, London for extracts in exercises 35 and 40 from *A History of Shopping* by D.Davis, 1966; Leonard Hill Books, Glasgow for an extract from *British Shopping Centres* by W.Burns, 1959; Hutchinson Publishing Group Ltd for an extract from *How We Lived Then* by Norman Longmate, 1971, (currently available in Arrow paperbacks); Penguin Books Ltd for the following extracts – from *The View in Winter: Reflections on Old Age* by Ronald Blythe (Allen Lane, 1979) pp. 118–125, copyright © Ronald Blythe, 1979, and from *Beside the Seaside* by James Walvin (Allen Lane, 1978) pp. 150–153, copyright © James Walvin, 1978; Longman Group Ltd for an extract from *Extinct and Vanishing Animals* by V.Ziswiler, 1967; Curtis Brown Ltd for an extract from *The Tomb of Tutankhamen* by Howard Carter; to the Historic Society of Lancashire and Cheshire for an extract from their *Transactions* 1953, Vol. 105, 1954; British Tourist Authority with *Country Life* for an extract from *Chapels and Churches: Who Cares?* by Marcus Binney and Peter Burman, 1977.